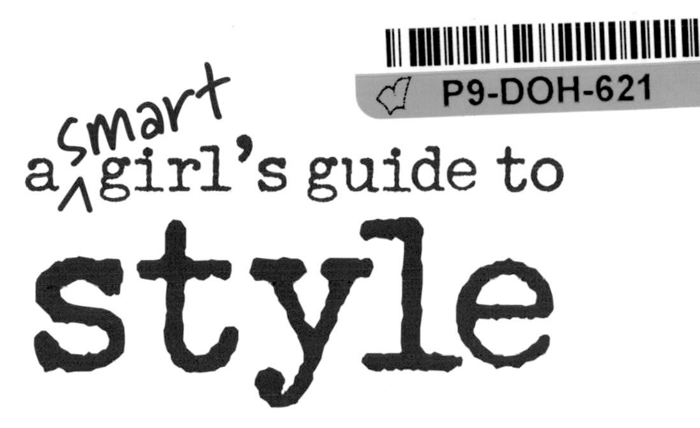

a smart girl's guide to style

how to have fun with fashion, shop smart, and let your personal style shine through

by Sharon Cindrich
illustrated by Shannon Laskey

American Girl®

Published by American Girl Publishing

Questions or comments? Call 1-800-845-0005, visit **americangirl.com**, or write to Customer Service, American Girl, 8400 Fairway Place, Middleton, WI 53562-0497.

Printed in China
12 13 14 15 16 17 18 LEO 11 10 9 8 7 6 5

Editorial Development: Erin Falligant, Kristi Thom
Art Direction and Design: Lisa Wilber, Chris Lorette David
Production: Tami Kepler, Sarah Boecher, Jeannette Bailey, Judith Lary

Photography, p. 43: satin—© iStockphoto/gmutlu; chiffon—© iStockphoto/Okea; taffeta—© iStockphoto/petermccue

Special thanks to Megan Boswell and to Victor Connors, optometrist at Isthmus Eye Care (Middleton, WI) and CEO of USA Optometry Giving Sight.

Dear Reader,

Every day, you make decisions about what to wear. Some mornings, you jump out of bed, grab something from your closet, and run out the door. Other days, you carefully choose something special or combine different clothes and accessories to create a whole new outfit.

Your parents used to choose your clothes for you, but now you know what you like—and you probably like making those decisions for yourself. You might notice the fashions hanging at the mall or the clothes that your friends are wearing. But every time you choose a shirt, slide a bracelet onto your wrist, or pull your hair back with a headband or barrette, you're expressing your own personal style.

This book is all about exploring your style. You'll take quizzes to help you figure out which looks make you feel comfortable and confident. You'll find tips for how to shop smart and talk with your parents about the clothes you want to buy and wear. And you'll get advice from other girls on how to ignore fashion critics and stay true to the styles you love.

You'll learn—if you haven't already—that style is about much more than clothes. It's about expressing your personality through the outfits you create. Just as your personality is unique, your style is, too. And it's changing and growing, just as you are. We hope this book will help you have fun with style and express the one-of-a-kind girl you are today.

Your friends at American Girl

contents

scarves
beads
rings
ribbons
swim gear
ballet stuff
tennis clothes
thermal socks
GIVEAWAY!

fashion vs. style

what's the difference?

You might not have thought about it before, but style and fashion are two different things. Fashion alone doesn't make a girl look or feel good. It's your own sense of style that plays the biggest part in how you present yourself to the world each day.

Fashion is an industry made up of businesses that make and sell clothing, shoes, jewelry, and lots of other things girls—and guys—like to wear. The fashion industry introduces new clothes and color combinations each season and promotes certain brands of clothing and accessories. Fashion is changing constantly, because new trends mean more sales for the industry. But that doesn't mean you have to "buy into" every fashion trend that comes along.

Style is a personal way of doing something. Style is *how* you wear that new shirt—buttoned and cinched with a belt or unbuttoned over a tank top. Style is all about the way you match up those leggings with a favorite skirt or combine a fun chunky bracelet with a simple blue dress. Style is your own unique approach—the combination of your personality, your creativity, and your confidence all wrapped up into one.

Fashion and style go hand in hand when it comes to choosing what you'll wear to school, to the park, or to a party. The fashions you see influence your style. Here's how:

The lead singer from a band you like starts a **fashion** trend by always wearing red shoes to match her red guitar.

This inspires you to pair your purple sneakers with a purple backpack and create your own **style**.

Fashion experts on television report that oversized sweaters are in this season.

You might add your own **style** with a fun belt over the sweater and a pair of matching earrings.

An ad in your sister's **fashion** magazine features a glittery designer tote bag.

With a little glitter and fabric glue, you apply your own glitzy **style** to a tote bag you haven't used in a while.

What's *your* style? Girls spend a lot of time finding a personal style. You might try on different clothes or shoes. You might page through magazines or experiment with hair clips. Your style can change from season to season and even from one day to the next, depending on your mood, the weather, or the events on your calendar.

How will you know when you've found a style that works for you? That's easy. A perfect style for you is one that makes you feel good about yourself. If you're feeling great when you walk out the door, there's a good chance you've found your style.

trend timeline

You've probably noticed that fashion changes over time—jeans with wide legs are popular one year, but the next year everyone is wearing jeans with a straight cut. The white sneakers that were the in thing last season are replaced with chunky boots the next.

1920s
Loose-fitting dresses with low sashes were in fashion.

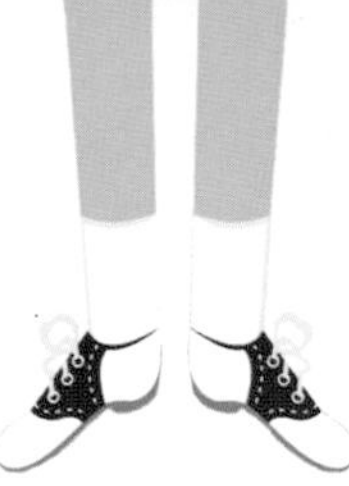

1950s
Girls wore poodle skirts, saddle shoes, and *monograms*—or initials—on their sweaters.

Exploring trends from the past can help give you a sense of just how much fashion has changed. And who knows? You might even find a little inspiration for your own style!

1970s
Bell-bottom jeans and tie-dye shirts were popular.

1990s
Girls dressed in oversized sweaters and mini skirts.

where do trends come from?

Fashion trends can come from:

a TV show whose popular characters always wear a certain kind of shoe.

a city where fashion designers work, such as Paris or New York.

a company that makes and sells fashion accessories, such as handbags.

a magazine that publishes articles about the fashion business and photos of people wearing different kinds of clothes.

Where do style trends come from? You, of course. And your friends. Style trends come from girls all over the country who add their own personal twists to the fashion trends they see. Finding fashion trends you like and applying your own creativity and personality to them is the best way to start developing your own sense of style.

There is no one in the world who has exactly your style—it is completely your own. That means that none of your classmates or friends can tell you how you should dress or express yourself. Exploring your own unique style takes courage and confidence.

trendsetter or fashion follower?

Answer these questions to find out if you tend to follow the styles of others or explore your own ideas with ease.

1. When it's time to choose a new pair of athletic shoes, you . . .
   a. **choose white like everyone else.**
   b. **pick a pair with a fashionable metallic stripe.**
   c. **are thrilled to find they come in orange—your favorite color!**

2. Your friends are all hoping for animal-print tote bags for their birthdays. You're hoping for . . .
   a. **an animal-print tote bag, of course—they're so cool!**
   b. **a tote bag made of recycled plastic—going green is cool!**
   c. **a felted bag you saw at a craft sale—handmade things are cool!**

3. You're heading for a haircut and preparing to tell the stylist what you want. You . . .
   a. **bring along a photo of your best friend. You want your hair to look just like hers.**
   b. **ask the stylist what looks are popular right now.**
   c. **describe to the stylist the one-of-a-kind look you're going for.**

4. Someone cracks a joke about the sequined pockets on your new jeans. You . . .

a. **take a survey of your friends, see what they think, and ask them if you should wear the jeans again.**

b. **pull out a magazine showing a celebrity wearing the *same* jeans.**

c. **shrug off the joke and walk tall—you love your new look!**

5. The school dance is coming. You really want something new to wear, but you don't have a lot of spending money. You . . .

a. **find out what your friends are wearing, and beg your parents to lend you the cash to buy the same thing.**

b. **scour discount stores for something that resembles the latest look.**

c. **take last year's dress, add a few accessories, and invent a totally fresh look.**

School Dance Friday!
School Dance Friday!
School D ce Friday!

Answers

Friend follower

If you answered mostly **a's,** you depend a lot on the attitudes and comments of friends when choosing what to wear. It can feel good to fit in, but don't let that desire hold you back from being your own girl. Gather the courage to try on your own style for size.

Trend tracker

If you answered mostly **b's,** you like exploring new trends but don't always fully express yourself for fear of sticking out. Looking to fashion trends for ideas isn't a problem. Just make sure you don't smother your own great creative style.

Style setter

If you answered mostly **c's,** you love finding new styles as much as sharing them with others. Being unique is something you savor, and you're not afraid to wear something you love even if no one else is wearing anything like it.

advice from girls

Here's what girls have to say about finding styles that match your mood, interests, and attitude.

Don't feel like you have to copy your friends. Set your own style, and maybe they'll copy YOU.

Try new colors. I just bought some purple shoes!

Look for clothes that fit your personality. After a while, you'll see a piece of clothing and be able to say, "Wow, that is so me."

Try on hand-me-downs from friends and family. Each person will have a different style.

girl style

These tips—inspired by girls' favorite outfits—may give you ideas for your *own* wardrobe.

Make patterns pop. Look for a plaid purse or polka-dot leggings.

Do you want to save the earth? Protect animals? Choose a shirt that'll help you spread the word!

Get creative with layers. Wear a skirt over jeans or a tank top over a shirt with longer sleeves.

Wear your favorite color from head to toe.

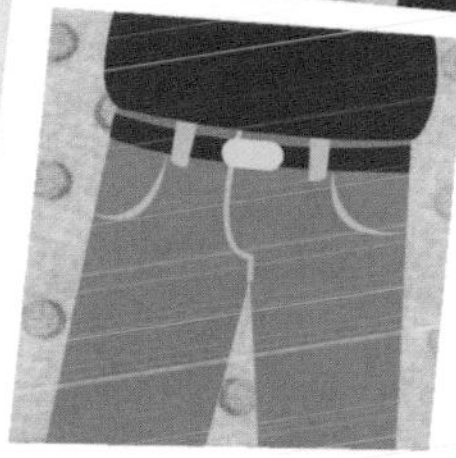

Mix and match patterns. Be brave, and have fun!

Dress up a sporty look with sparkly jewelry or a bright headband.

big truth

There is one part of style that you can't buy from a store or a catalogue, and that's your attitude. The way you hold your body when you walk down the hall, the words you use to communicate with others, and the choices you make each day are a big part of your personal style.

Staying positive, respecting others, and having confidence in yourself will help your style shine through. Not only will you feel good about how you look on the outside, you'll feel great about the person you are becoming on the inside, too.

the basics

fashion fundamentals

Chances are you've been noticing other girls' fashion choices. Maybe your friend got a cool new jacket for her birthday. Or the girl who sits in front of you at school has a great collection of sweaters. Or your best friend wears lots of bright colors.

As you begin to notice fashion and explore your own style, take a closer look at the basics in your closet—your shirts, sweaters, pants, shorts, skirts, and jeans. This is where your style starts, with the clothes that you mix and match every day.

"Basic" doesn't have to mean boring. Shirts come in dozens of styles and fabrics, and so do pants and sweaters. Dresses and skirts come in different lengths. And the combinations are endless.

As you learn about different kinds of clothing, think about how they feel on you and how you might wear them. That can help you look at your own style—and maybe even your own closet—in a whole new way.

HISTORY
BIOLOGY
SCIENCE
FRENCH
No1
CAL
G

shirts & sweaters

Shirts and sweaters come in a ton of **silhouettes** (sil-uh-WETS), or styles. They can have long sleeves, short sleeves, or no sleeves. They can slip over your head, button up the front, or wrap around your shoulders. Which of these styles do you like to wear?

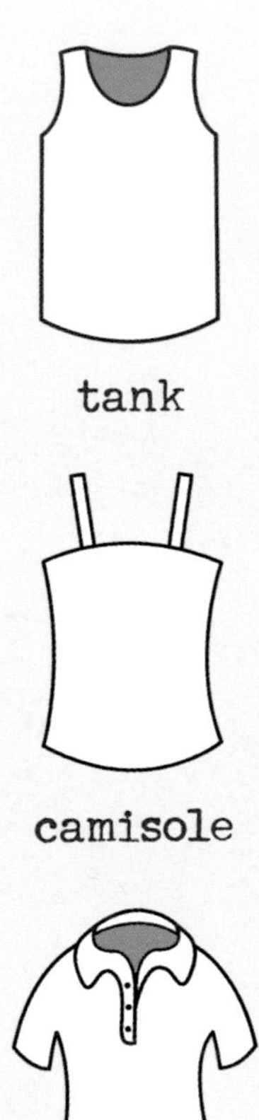

tank

halter

camisole

T-shirt

polo

henley

Did you know?
In England, sweaters are called "jumpers."

button-down

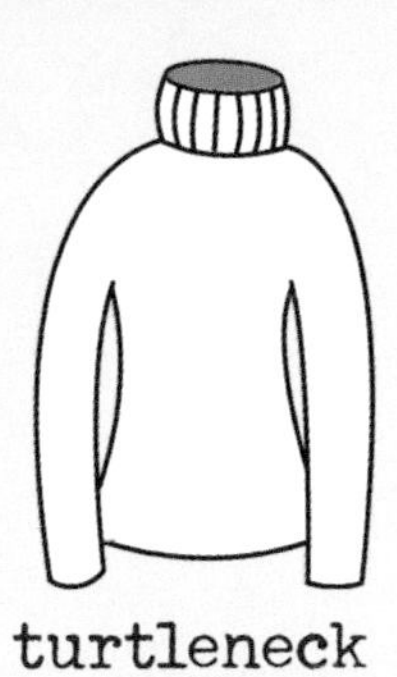

turtleneck

cardigan

pullover

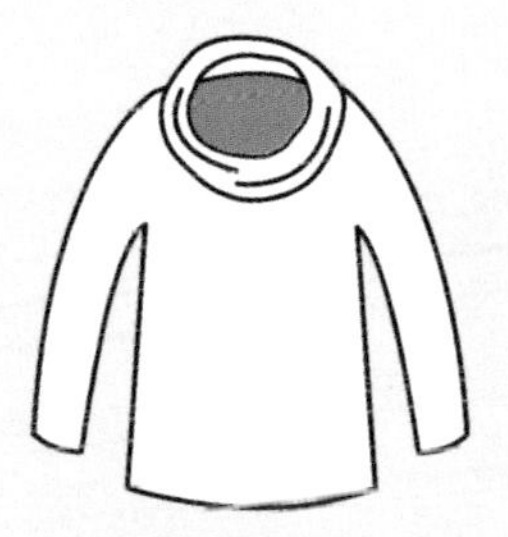

cowl-neck

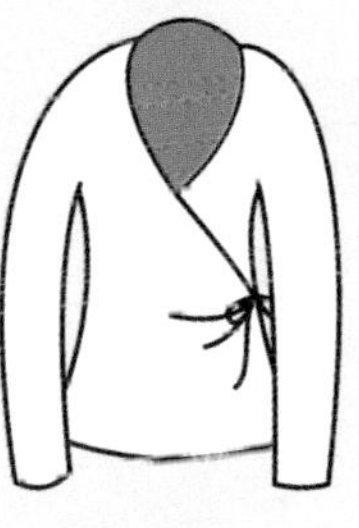

wrap

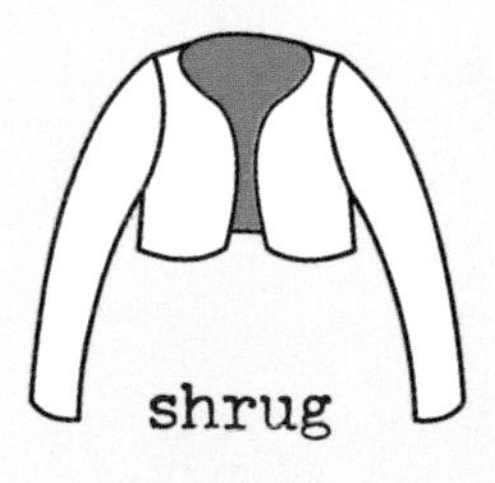

shrug

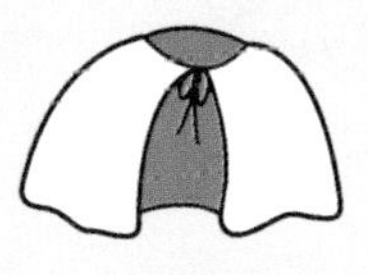

capelet

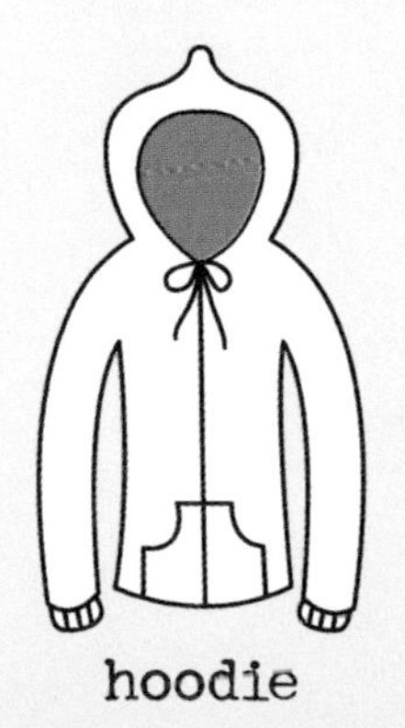

hoodie

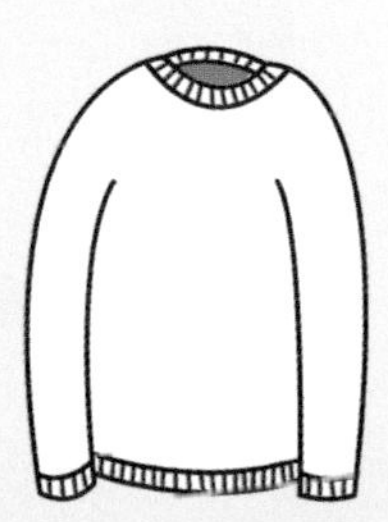

sweatshirt

collars, sleeves & necklines

How a shirt covers your neck and arms makes a big difference in the way the style looks. See for yourself.

Collars

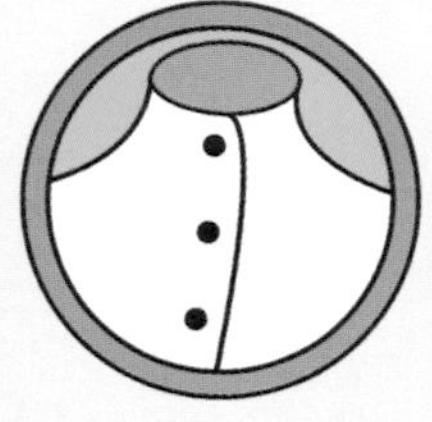

funnel neck

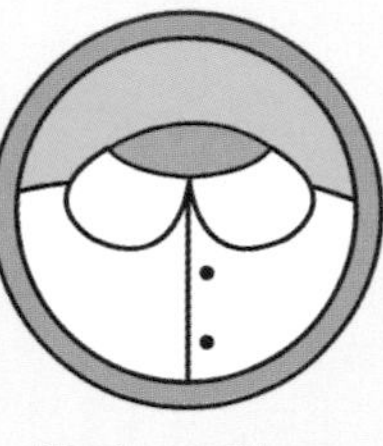

Peter Pan

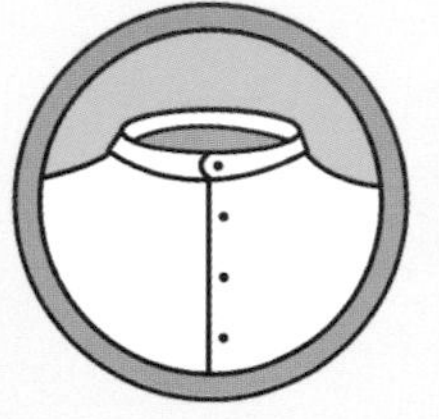

band

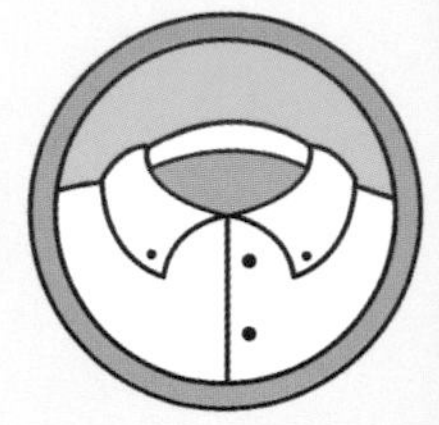

button-down

Sleeves

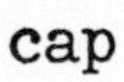

cap

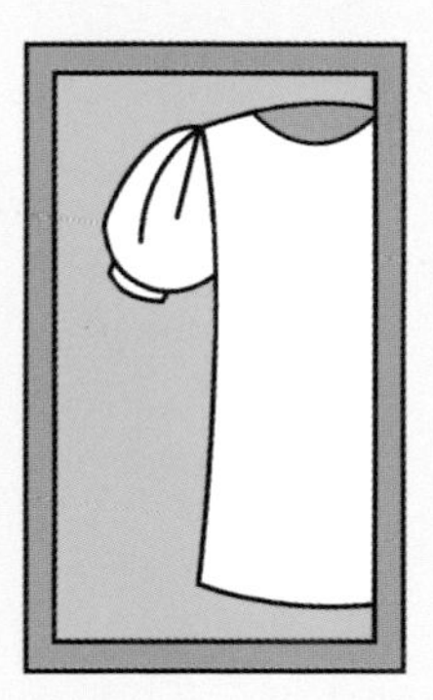

puff

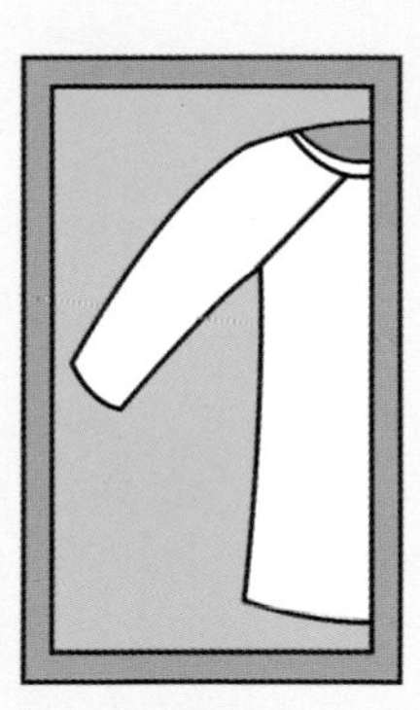

raglan

bell

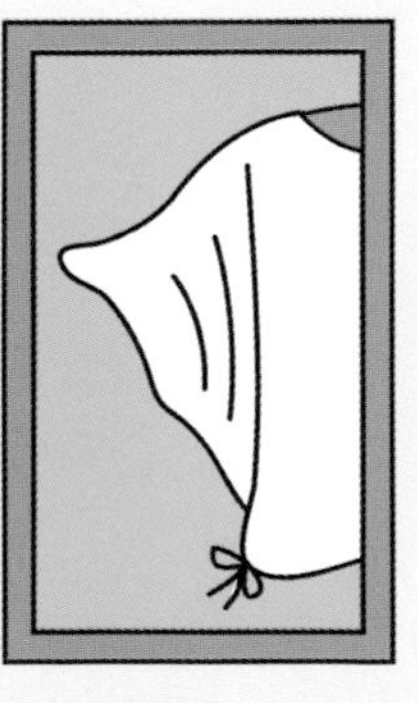

batwing

Necklines

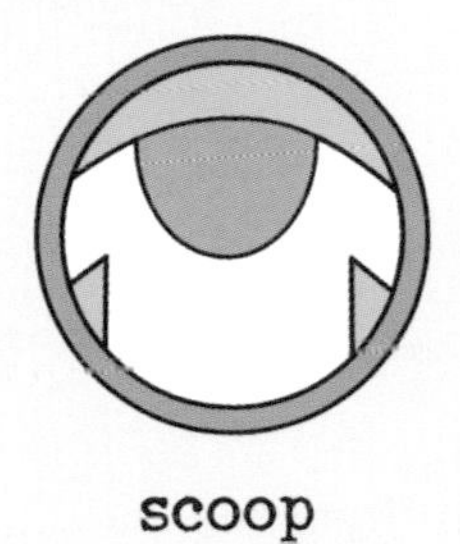

scoop

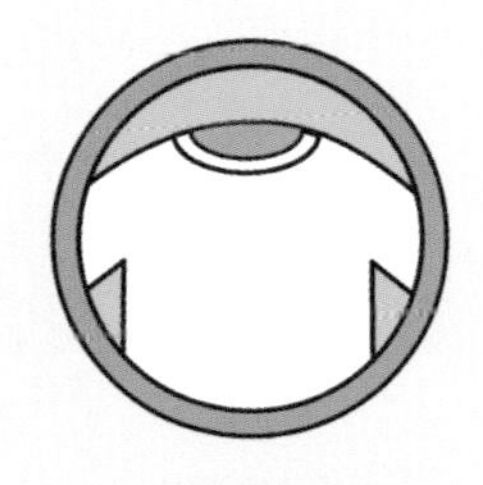

crew

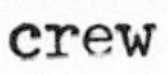

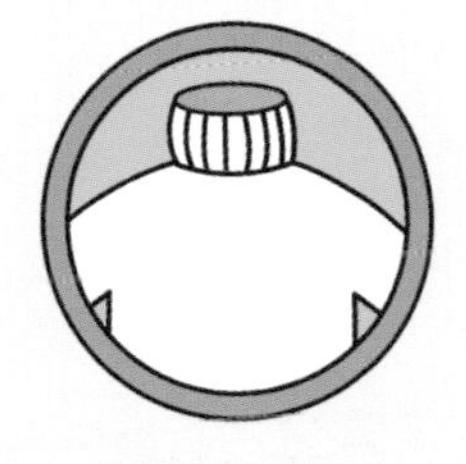

turtle

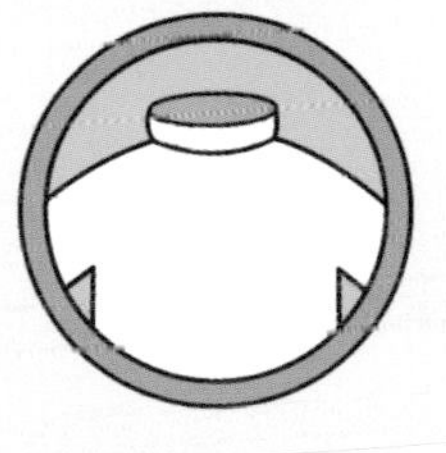

mock

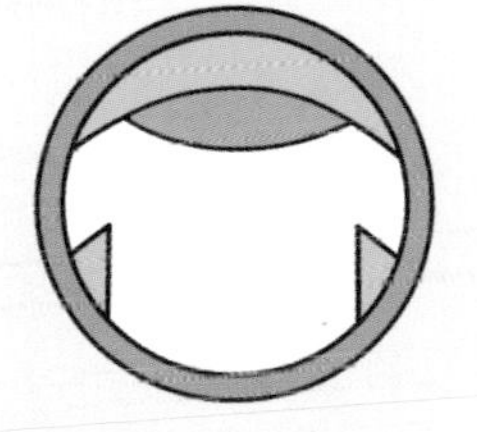

boat or bateau (bah-TOH)

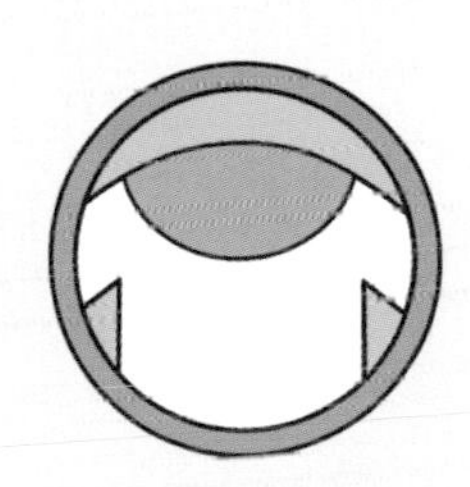

ballet

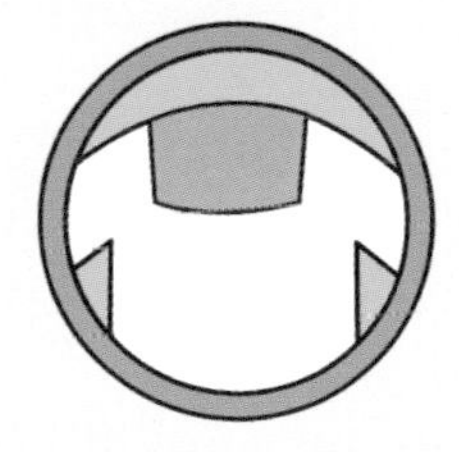

square

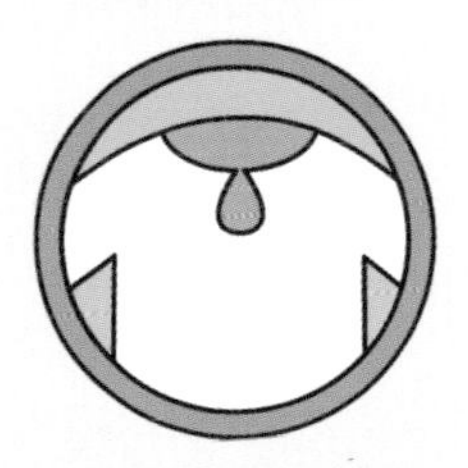

keyhole

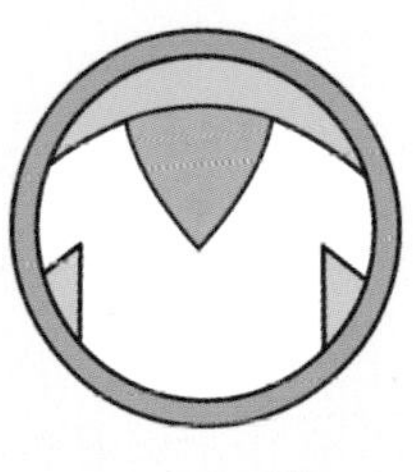

v-neck

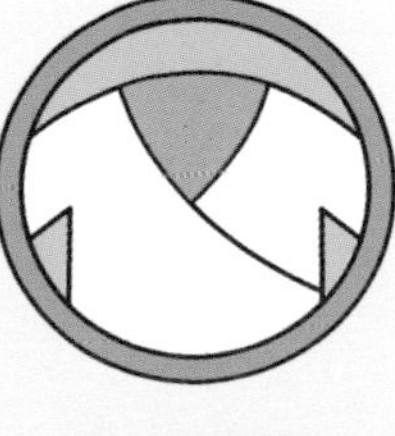

crossover

pants & shorts

Which bottoms fit your style?

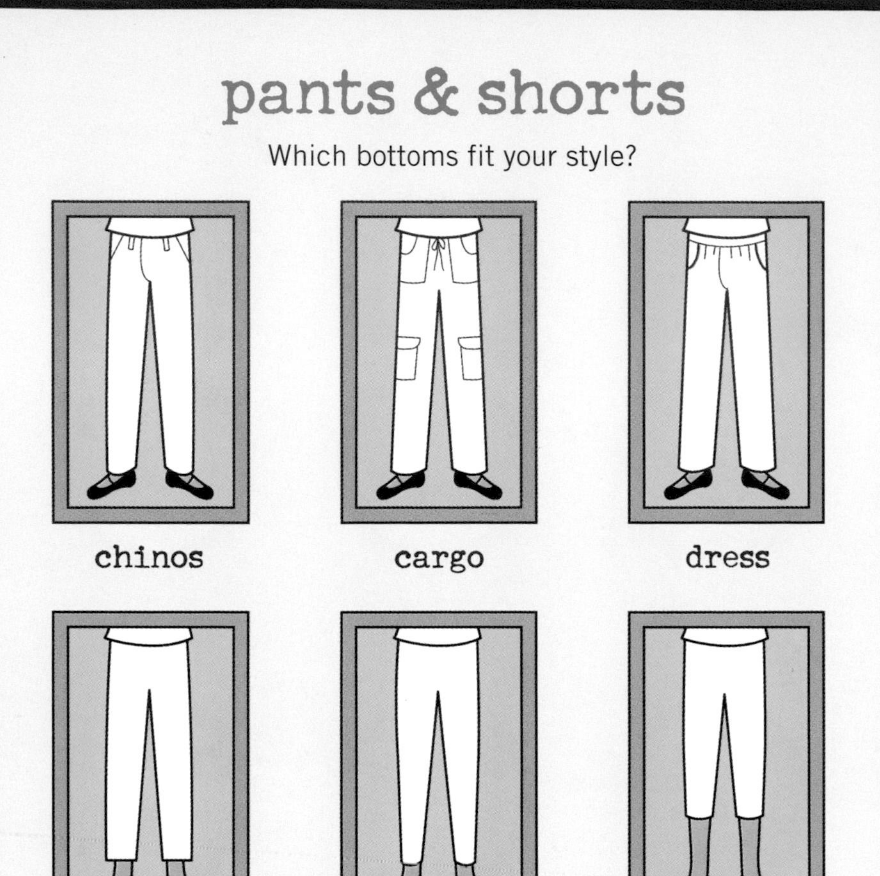

did you know?

Capri pants go by many names. In the 1950s, girls and women called them "pedal pushers" because the short pants wouldn't get caught in bicycle chains or wheels. And cuffed capris have been called "clam diggers" because people collecting clams in shallow water rolled up their pant legs to keep them from getting wet.

Jeans come in all sorts of styles, too.
Which of these are in your closet?

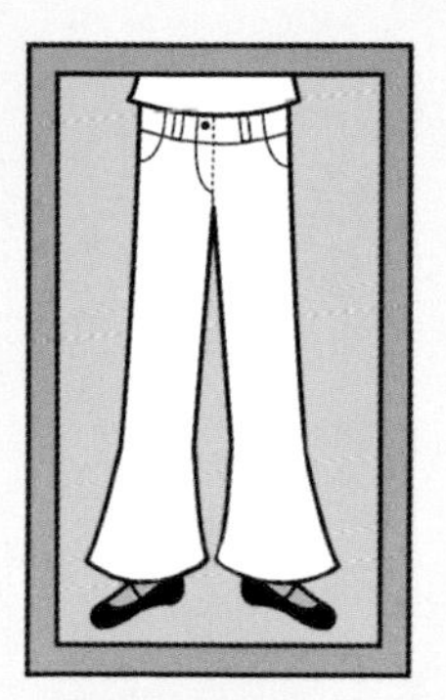

flared

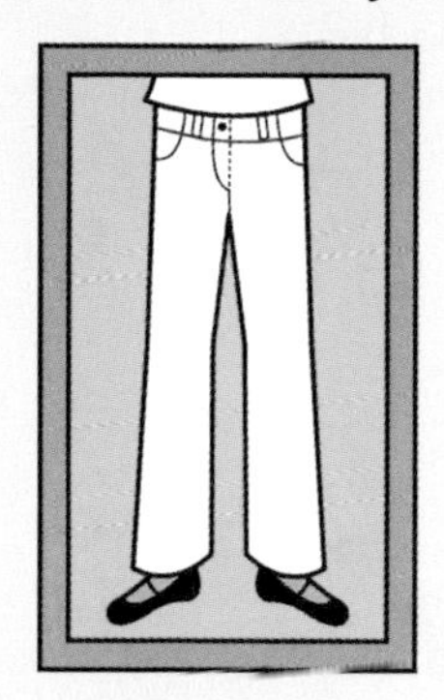

boot-cut

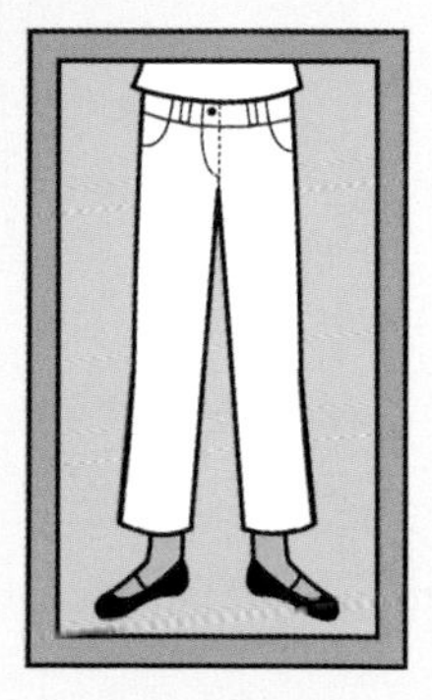

cropped

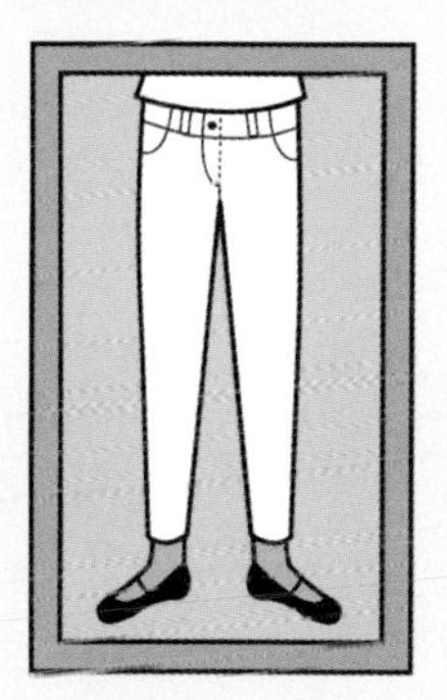

skinny-leg

trouser-style

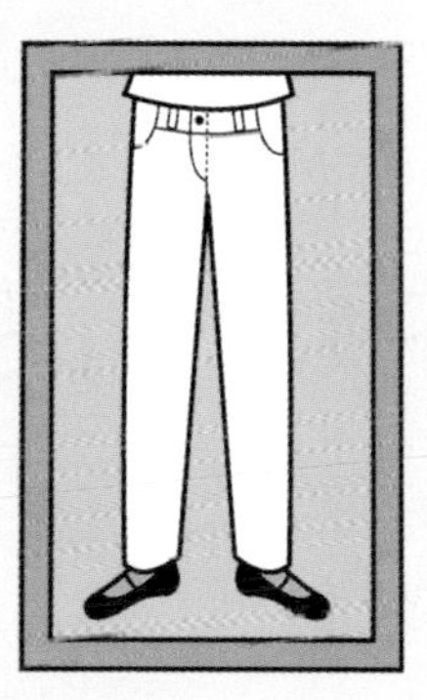

straight-leg

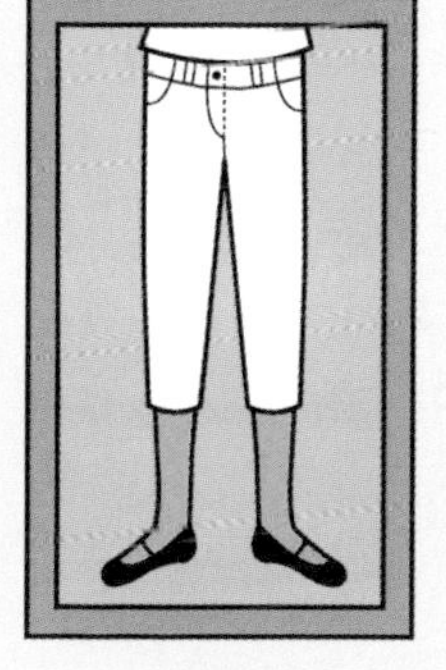

capris

trendy tip

Are your jeans getting too short? Before you get rid of them, consider rolling them up to a capri length. You'll preserve the jeans you love and add a "new" piece to your wardrobe.

skirts & dresses

Some skirts and dresses are best for special occasions, such as a school graduation or wedding. Other skirts and dresses are casual, such as the jean skirt you might put on for a trip to the mall. Which of these styles would you love to wear?

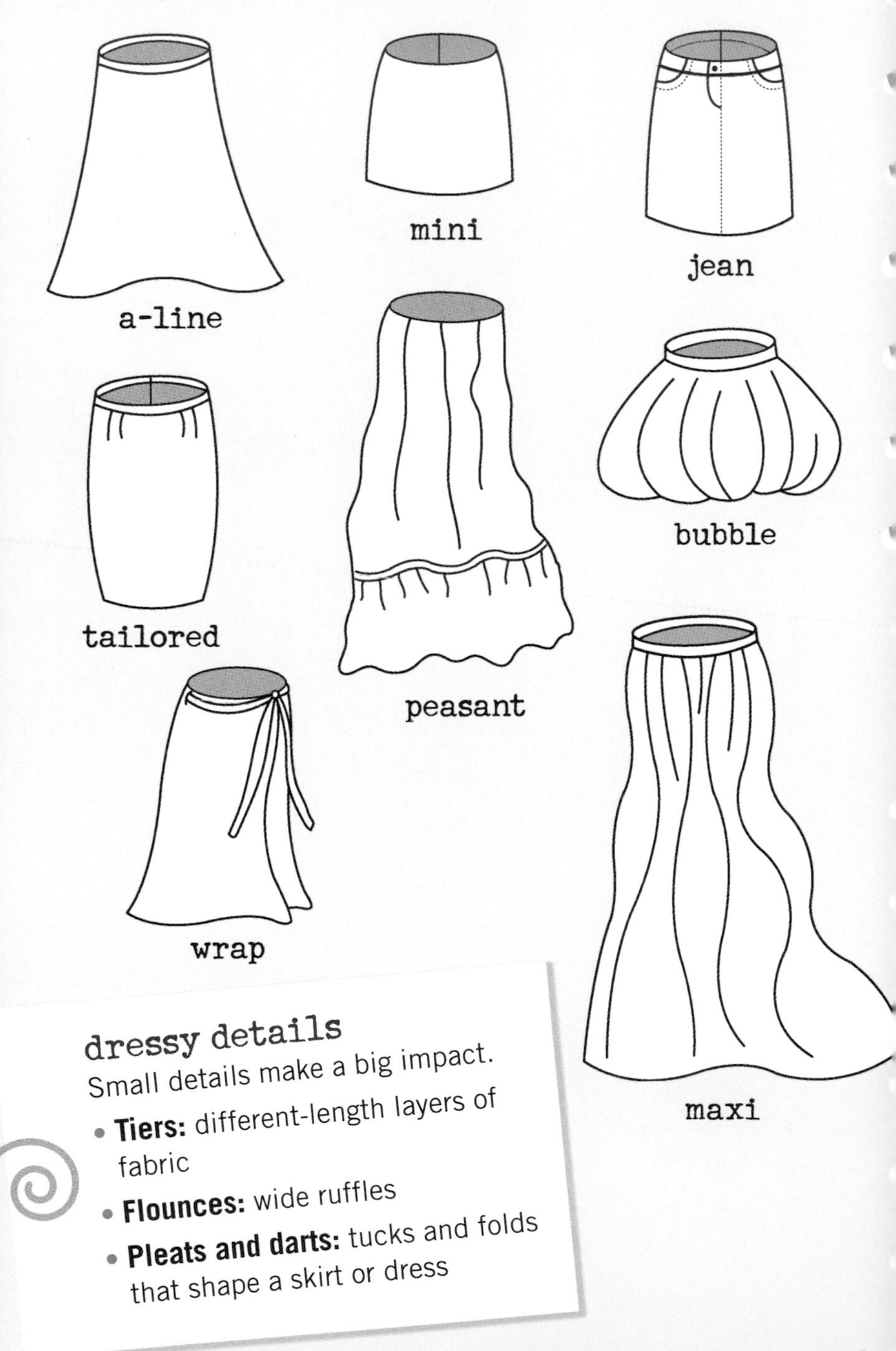

dressy details

Small details make a big impact.

- **Tiers:** different-length layers of fabric
- **Flounces:** wide ruffles
- **Pleats and darts:** tucks and folds that shape a skirt or dress

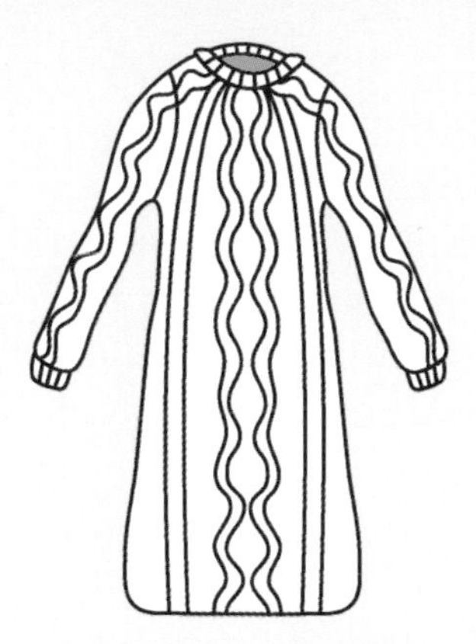

sweater dress

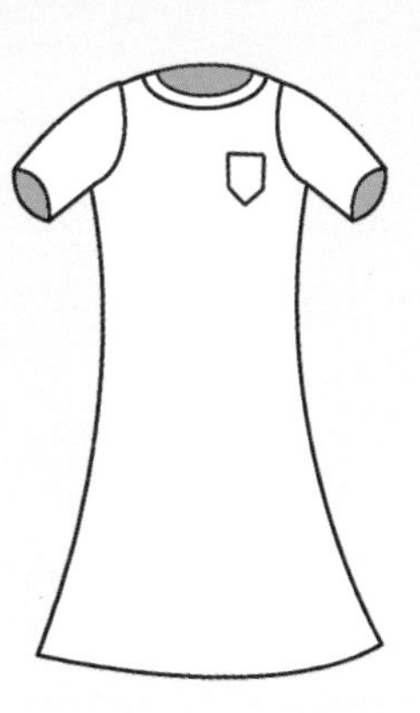

T-shirt dress

party dress

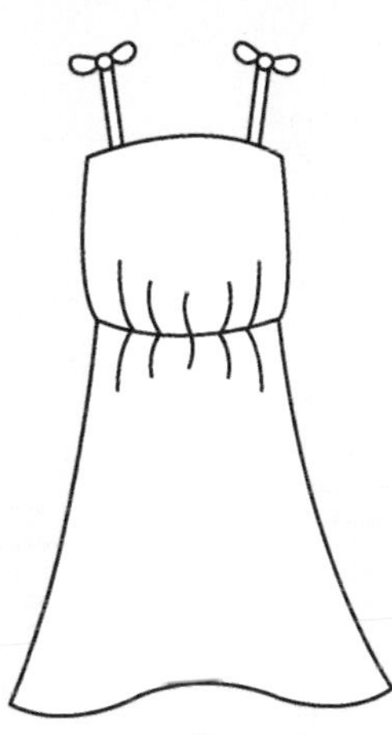

sundress

jumper

wonder about waistlines?

Your own waist stays in the same place, right around your belly button. But sometimes the waistline of clothing falls above or below your waist to create a particular look, as in these styles:

- **Empire** (AHM-peer) **waist:** sits high above your waist, around your ribs
- **Drop waist:** hits below your waist at or above your hips
- **Basque** (bask) **waist:** dips into a V below your waist

socks, bras & underwear

Underwear may not seem to matter to your style—after all, no one can see it, right? But underwear does play an important role. It protects your body from fabrics and seams that can irritate your skin. Underwear and socks absorb sweat, which can make your clothes and shoes smell bad. Long underwear can keep you warm during outdoor winter activities. And underwear provides an extra layer of covering in case a button pops, pants rip, or a skirt blows up in the wind. If you're comfortable, clean, and covered, you'll feel good about yourself. That's the most important part of any style you choose.

When you're selecting your underwear, think about patterns and colors that might show through your clothes. These tips can help you make good choices:

Undershirts and camisoles. Wear one of these under a shirt or sweater that might be *sheer*, or see-through.

Bras. Wear a skin-colored bra under white blouses and T-shirts. Are your bra straps showing? Check with your mom to make sure that your bra fits properly and that the straps are snug. If your straps still peek out from the neckline or sleeves of your shirt, layer a tank top or camisole over your bra.

Panties. Save patterned undies for jeans and dark pants so that prints don't show through.

Slips. If your skirt is sheer, a slip will keep you covered. If you're wearing tights, a slip will also keep your skirt from clinging to your tights.

Socks and tights. Here's where you can play with patterns. Striped tights or over-the-knee socks look great under a solid-colored skirt.

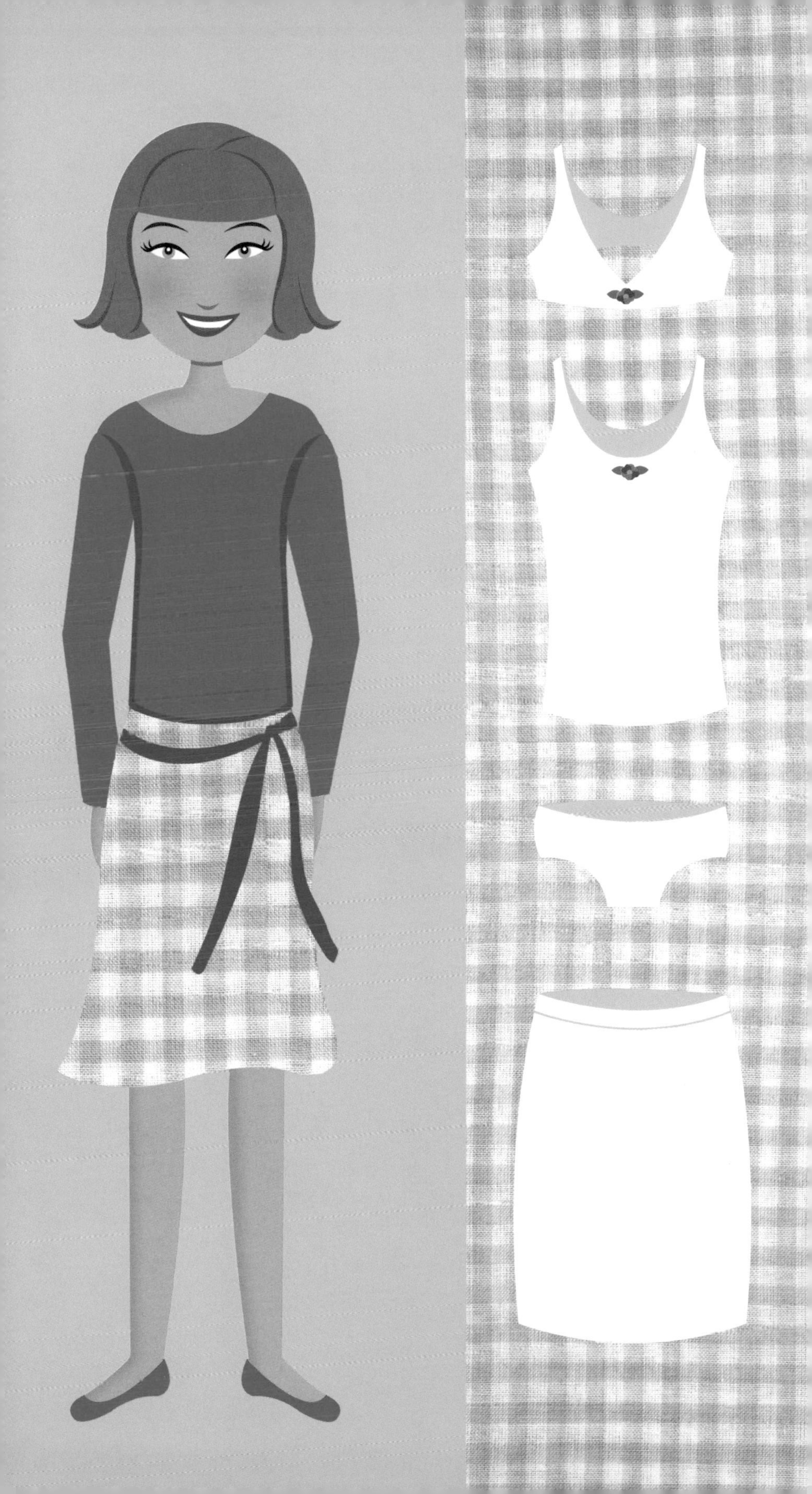

coats & jackets

Worried about covering up your style? Don't be! Coats, ponchos, and raincoats can all be fashionable. Which of these would complement the clothes you wear?

puffer

peacoat

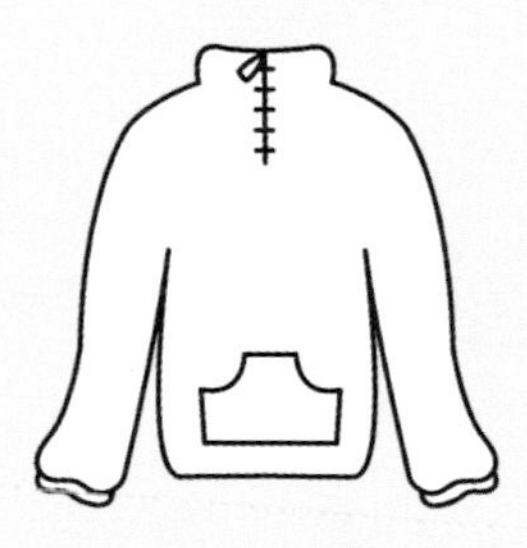

fleece pullover

blazer

dress coat

parka

did you know?

The inspirations for many outdoor garments come from other cultures. For instance, ponchos came from South America, and parkas were worn by nomads in the coldest areas of Russia.

athletic jacket

jean jacket

trench coat

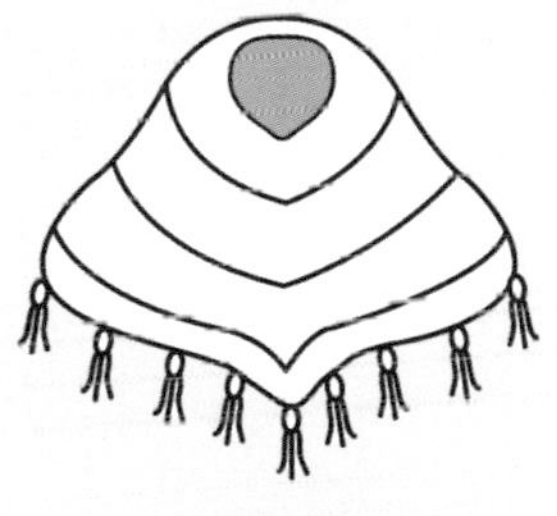
poncho

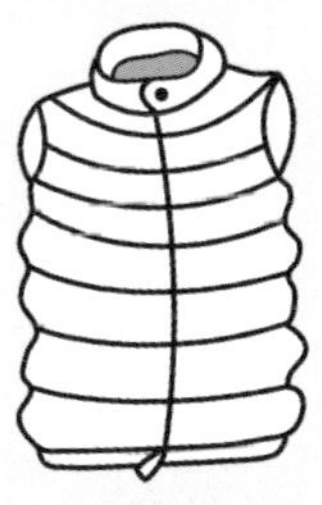
vest

ski jacket

windbreaker

mix & match

Mixing and matching some of the clothing you already own is a fun and inexpensive way to create new looks. Pull out ten pieces of clothing from your closet, following the checklist below. (If you don't have something on the list, just grab two of something else.) Make sure that at least half of the items are solid, neutral colors, such as black, dark blue, white, or tan.

Now, start experimenting to find some fun new combinations. Pair a tank top with jeans and a cardigan. Put a T-shirt over a short skirt, and add a pair of leggings. Mix colors that you might not have thought would go together, too. How's it going? How many combinations can you create? Ask a friend or sibling to snap photos of you in the outfits you like. That way you'll remember them and can wear them again.

what to wear?

A key part of having style is knowing what to wear—and when. Circle the answers below that sound like outfits you'd choose.

1. It's the first day of school, and the weather report calls for chilly, rainy weather. You wear . . .

   a. the skirt and sandals you had planned on. A few raindrops won't stop you from enjoying your back-to-school outfit.

   b. leggings and boots instead. You cross your fingers that tomorrow will be sunny, sandal-wearing weather.

   c. your worn-out jeans and sneakers. You may not stay completely dry, but at least you'll be comfortable.

2. Your friend Bailey called and invited you to a party at her place on Friday night. She's invited five other friends over to watch movies and play games. You wear . . .

   a. a satin skirt with red flats and your gold locket—you've been looking for an excuse to get dressed up.

   b. jeans and a sparkly T-shirt cinched with a funky pink belt. It's a look you've been wanting to try.

   c. sweatpants and a sweatshirt. If the party turns into a sleepover, you'll be all set!

3. Your grandpa is retiring from his job, and your family has been invited to an awards banquet. You wear . . .

   a. the silk kimono your grandparents brought back for you from their trip to Japan.

   b. a skirt and the shell bracelet your grandparents brought you from Hawaii.

   c. Your lucky pair of jeans and the T-shirt your grandparents brought you from Costa Rica.

4. Picture day is tomorrow, and you're choosing an outfit. You decide to wear . . .

   a. the dress you wore in your aunt's wedding. Maybe your mom can re-create your hairdo from that day, too.

   b. a nice pair of jeans and your green pullover sweater. Green matches your eyes.

   c. a sweatshirt and sweatpants in your school colors. You want to show your school spirit.

5. Your best friend, Shelby, called and invited you to go out to eat with her family. Reservations at the restaurant are for 7:00, so she says she'll pick you up at 6:45. That's only 20 minutes from now. Yikes! You wear . . .

   a. your holiday dress and a sparkly headband.

   b. your blue T-shirt dress and boots.

   c. exactly what you have on—a sports jersey from your favorite team and a pair of sneakers.

Answers

Fancy Fiona

If you answered mostly **a's,** you treat any invitation as an excuse to wear your fanciest fashions. You're all set for formal occasions like wedding receptions and holiday parties, but what happens when you show up at an outdoor birthday party and you're way overdressed? You might have to sit out on some of the fun or risk ruining your best clothes. Save them for formal or *semi-formal* occasions, such as school dances, concerts, and church services. If the occasion calls for casual, don't stress—you can dress up even the most casual of outfits with some fun jewelry and hair accessories.

Practical Peyton

If you answered mostly **b's,** you're smart about knowing what to wear when. You know that before you hit your closet, you need to consider the weather and the kinds of things you'll be doing that day. Your fashion sense may save you from feeling overdressed or underdressed—and might save your best clothes from wear and tear, too. Just be sure that when you *can* wear your dressy clothes, you do. Otherwise, you might discover you've outgrown them without having had the chance to enjoy them!

Casual Chloe

If you answered mostly **c's,** you're all about being comfortable, no matter what the occasion. That's great when you're hanging out at home or with a friend, but there's nothing comfortable about showing up at a party or restaurant where the dress code calls for fancier clothes than what you've got on. If you're not sure what the dress code is, ask. Or follow your parents' advice. They'll know what's appropriate, especially when it comes to formal events. Just make sure that you've got at least one dressy outfit hanging in your closet for those occasions when you'll need it.

quick change

Do you love that tank top but think it's too cold outside to go without sleeves? Try these seasonal solutions to enjoy your favorite pieces all year long.

Tank-top tweaks. Wear a tank top over a long-sleeved shirt or under a cardigan sweater.

Short but sweet. Wear a mini skirt over a pair of leggings.

Short-sleeved tees. Layer one of these over a long-sleeved T-shirt.

Sundress switch. Wear a sundress over leggings or jeans and a long-sleeved T-shirt or sweater.

fun with fabrics

What makes clothing stiff or soft? Shiny or dull? Fuzzy or scratchy? It's fabric—the material that makes up your clothes. Different fabrics can completely change the look, feel, and design of clothing. For instance, the same style of shirt can be made of silk (something you'd wear to a concert or a nice restaurant) or fleece (something you'd wear around the house to keep you warm).

Discovering fabrics you like and combining them with looks you love is a great way to explore your style. Touch and try on a few of these:

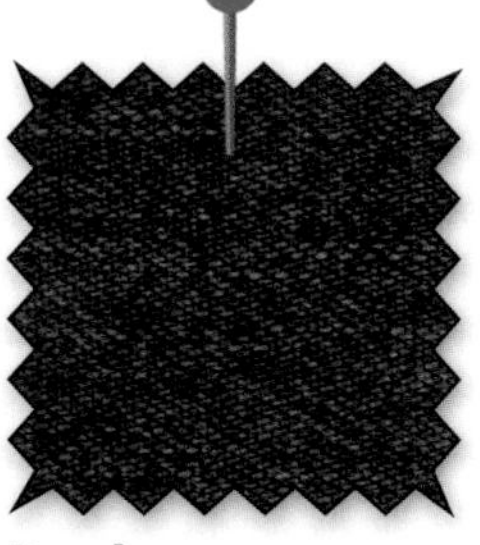

Denim—a sturdy, heavyweight cotton fabric used for making jeans

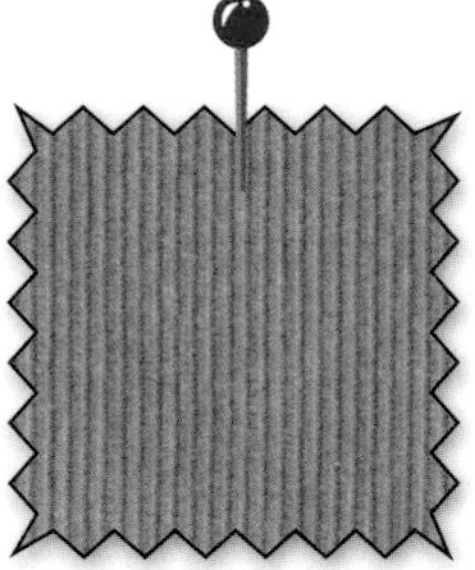

Corduroy—a textured material made up of vertical rows of tufted fabric

Jersey—a soft knit fabric used for T-shirts, leggings, pajamas, and underwear

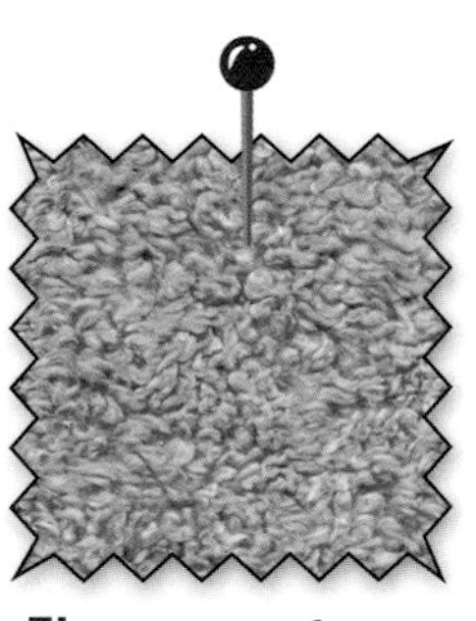

Fleece—a fuzzy, warm fabric

Did you know?
The word *scroop* is used in the fashion industry to describe the rustling sound some fabrics make when they are handled.

Satin—a shiny fabric that's smooth to the touch

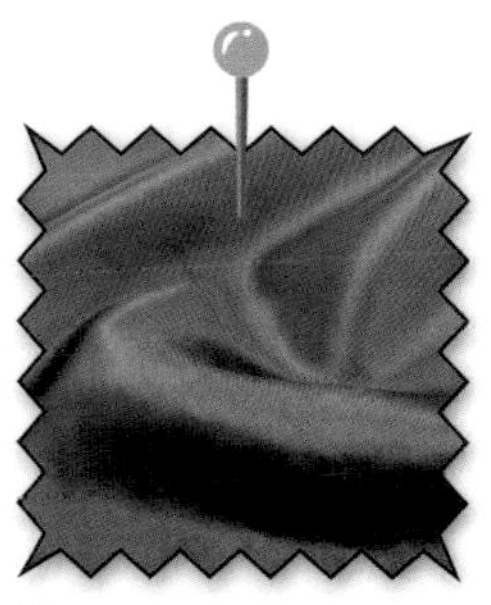

Taffeta—a crisp, shiny fabric used to make dressy garments

Tulle (tool)—a stiff mesh netting used as trim or as an over- or underlayer in dressy styles

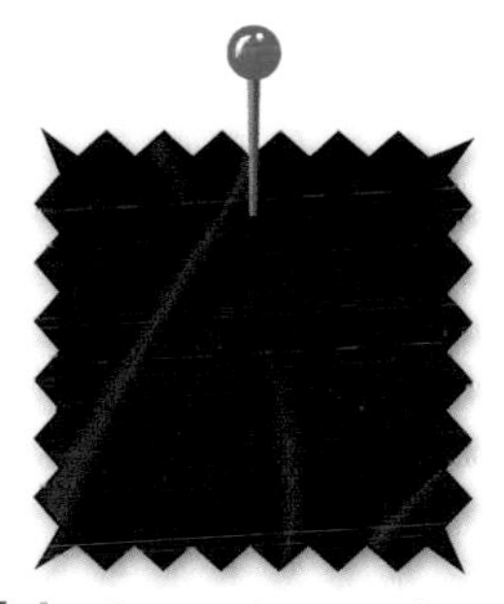

Velvet—a dense, fuzzy fabric that feels extra soft

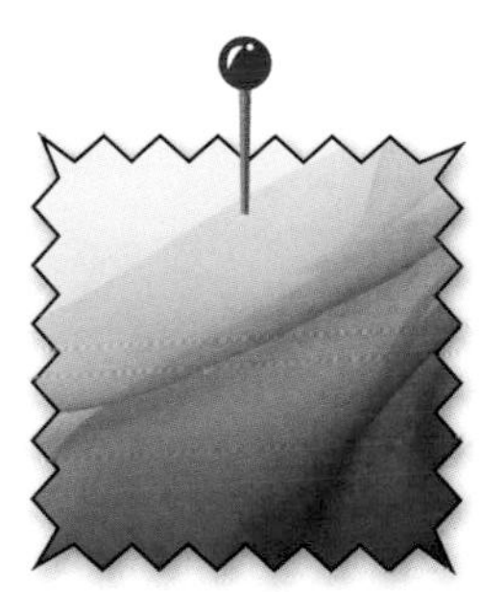

Chiffon (shif-AHN)—a sheer, lightweight, drapey fabric

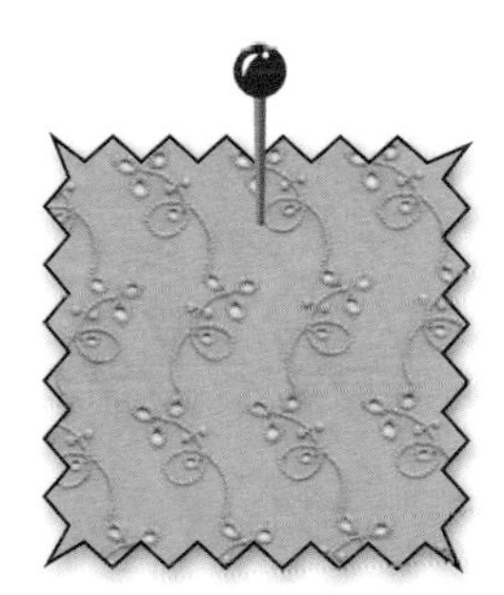

Eyelet—usually a cotton fabric with small holes embroidered with a lacy pattern

Tag, you're it!

How can you find out what your clothes are made of? Look inside. Tags sewn inside your clothing will not only help you identify the fabric content but will also give instructions on how to clean it. Not every fabric can be thrown into your washing machine—some require hand washing or dry cleaning. And some fabrics, like wool, might make you feel itchy. Reading tags will help you make good choices when it comes to your clothes.

patterns & prints

Not only are fabrics made of different fibers and weaves, but they also come in a variety of patterns and prints. *Patterns* are woven into the fabric. *Prints* are applied to the surface of the fabric, so you may see the design on only one side. Which of these do you like best?

Patterns

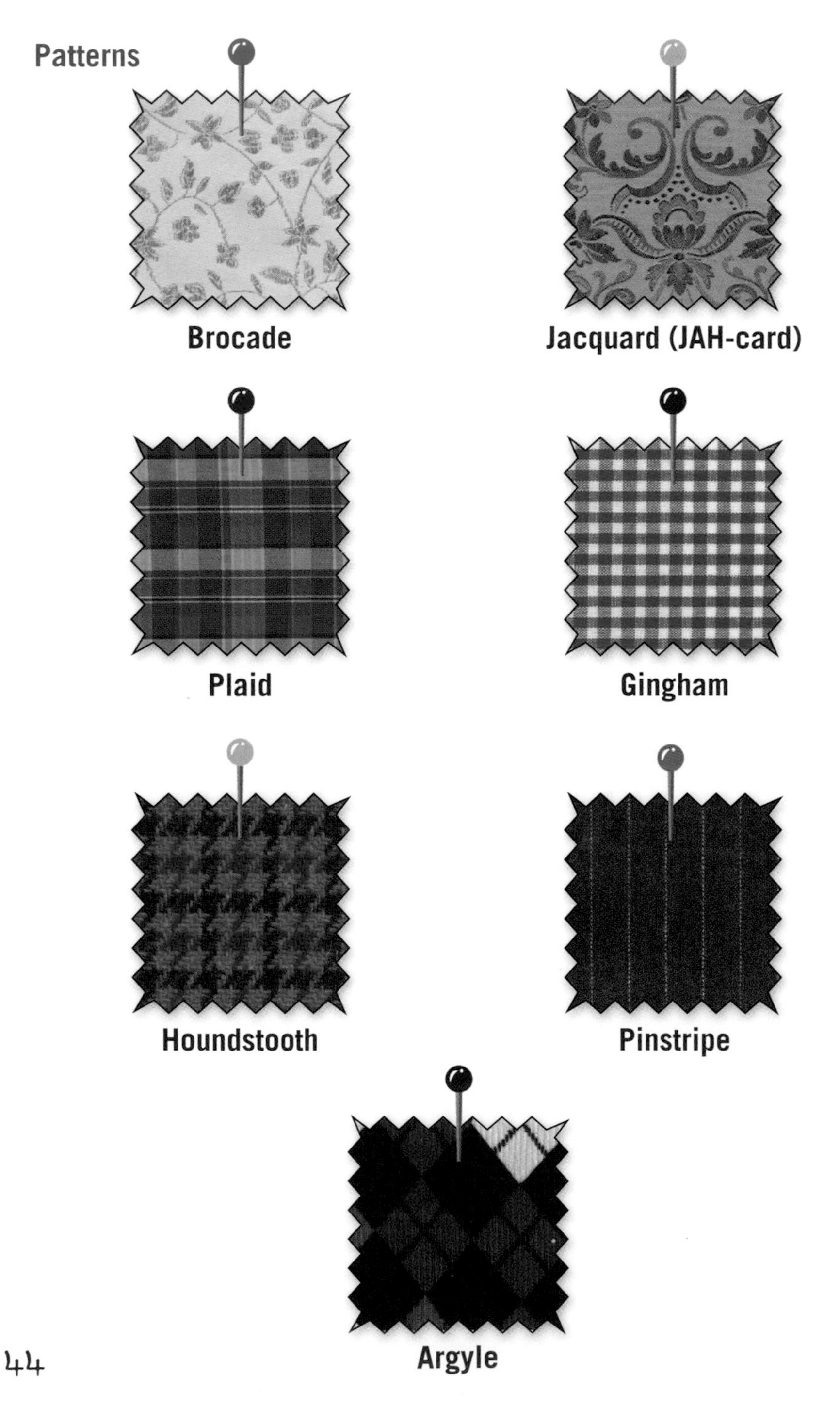

Prints

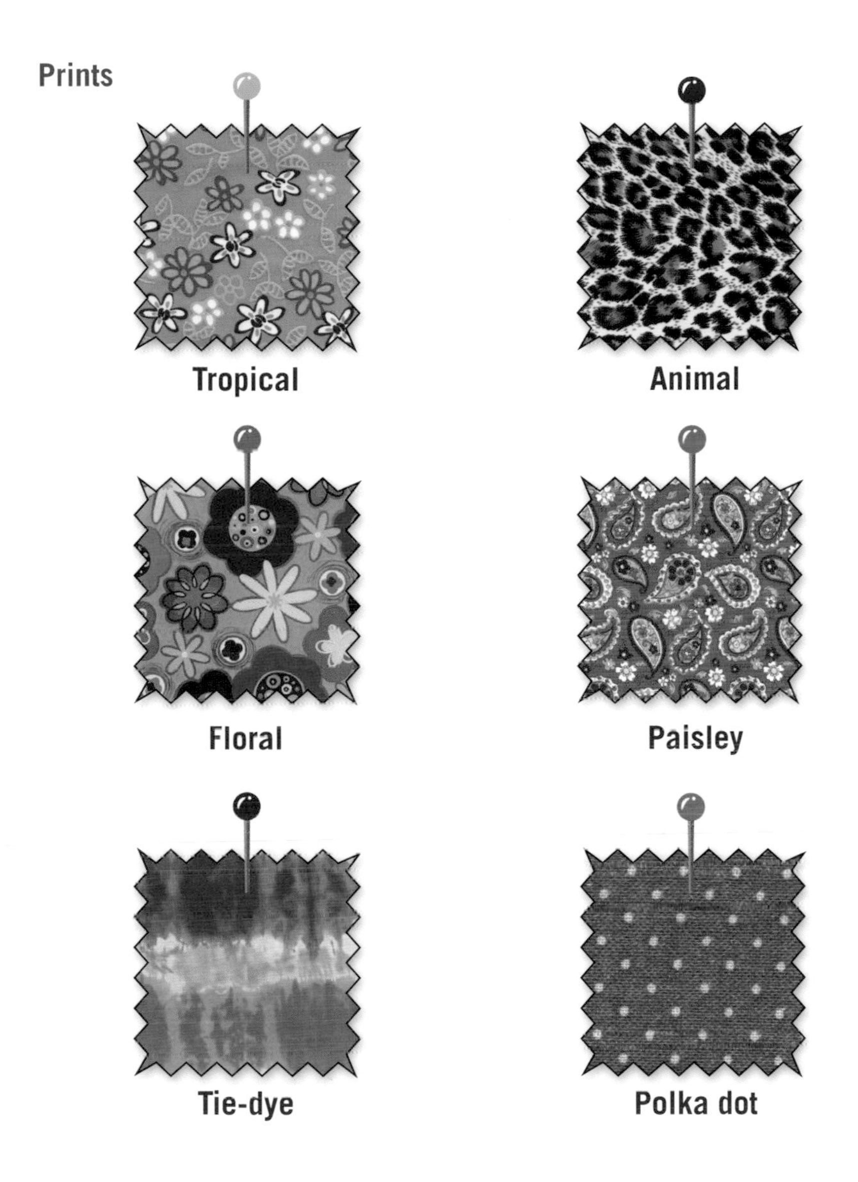

Pairing patterns

To mix and match the patterns and prints that you love most, try these tips:

- Pair a large, bold pattern or print with a smaller, simpler one.
- Pair a couple of patterns or prints with one solid piece of clothing, such as a plain white T-shirt or a black skirt.
- Try putting together patterns and prints that are the same color or in the same color family, such as blues and purples.

quiz

crazy for one color?

Answer these questions to find out.

1. You need a new sweater. The boutique in your town has only one sweater in your favorite color, and it's a size too big. You . . .

   a. buy it anyway. The color is more important than the fit.

   b. buy another color. As long as the sweater fits, it'll look great in any color.

2. When you open your closet door, you see . . .

   a. a lot of one color.

   b. a rainbow of colors.

3. The new scarf you got for your birthday is a combination of orange, yellow, and green. You . . .

   a. sigh. You wish it were a color you wear more often.

   b. start thinking about all the different pieces in your closet that can go with this funky new accessory.

4. Your family is moving, and your new room has white walls. You . . .

   a. decide to paint your walls pink to match your pink bedding and pink lamp.

   b. paint your walls green to complement your pink bedding and pink lamp.

5. Your winter coat has always been blue, so when it's time to buy a new one, you . . .

   a. buy another blue one. It goes perfectly with your blue hat and scarf.

   b. decide to try something new. A purple coat goes with your blue winter accessories, too.

Answers

True blue

If you answered mostly **a's,** you feel a special attachment to a particular color. There's nothing wrong with surrounding yourself with the color that you love. When you need a pick-me-up, though, a splash of a new color can brighten your room, wardrobe, and mood.

Color lover

If you answered mostly **b's,** you like many different colors and look for opportunities to try new shades. Consider organizing your closet by color—all blue shirts in one place, all pink shirts together, and so on. That way, you'll quickly spot the hue to suit your mood.

Would you like to add more color to your outfits? Check out the color combinations below. If you love your purple T-shirt, add a blue headband. Or wear your green hoodie unzipped over a yellow tank top. Pairing coordinating colors makes both colors pop.

trying new tints

Just because you don't like how you look in a certain navy blue sweater doesn't mean that blue isn't a good color on you. Try aqua, turquoise, cornflower blue, or sky blue. You might need to try a lot of shades of a color to find the ones that flatter you most.

When trying new colors, follow these tips:

- Try on colors in a room with good lighting to see the true hue.
- Try one color at a time with a solid, neutral-colored pair of pants (such as black, blue, or tan) to get a real feel for the shade.
- Try on colors you don't normally wear, and ask your mom or a friend for her opinion on which ones look best on you.
- Try on clothing in a color that matches your eyes. Chances are, it'll be a flattering color for you.

In the end, your opinion matters most. If wearing a certain color makes you feel good about yourself, it's a great choice.

what do you do?

You try to put together a great look and take care of your clothes and accessories, but unexpected things happen. Here's how to handle fashion emergencies with calm and common sense.

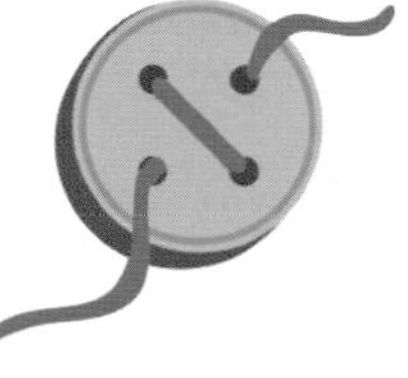

In the middle of class, a button pops off your shirt!

Stay cool. Wait for a break in class, and then tell your teacher what happened. Ask if you can go to your locker and get a sweater or sweatshirt to change into. If you don't have a change of clothes, go to the school office and ask for a safety pin. Pin your shirt closed, and then forget about it. Fiddling with the pin will just draw more attention to it.

As you grab your spiral notebook out of your backpack, the metal spiral snags your sweater.

Don't panic. Carefully unhook the metal spiral from your sweater. If you can, gently tuck the snagged thread back through the sweater. If you can't, ask your teacher for a small piece of clear tape, and put it over the snag to avoid catching it again. When you get home, a parent can help you pull the snag back inside the sweater.

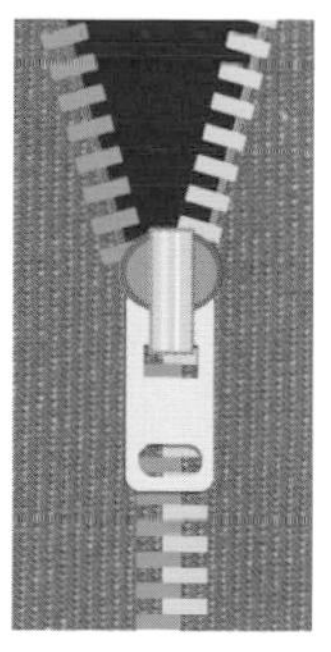

After a trip to the bathroom, you can't get the zipper on your jeans to work.

Take a deep breath. If you're still in the bathroom stall, take off your jeans to get a better look at the problem. Look to see if a string or small piece of denim is stuck in the zipper's path. If that's not the problem, jiggle the zipper a bit, moving the zipper pull down first and then gently up again a few times. If the zipper is still stuck, put your pants back on, button or snap them at the waist, and pull your shirt down over the zipper. Shirt not long enough? Ask a friend if she can lend you a sweater or sweatshirt to tie around your waist. Or ask a teacher for a safety pin, and pin the gap closed till you get home.

During recess, you accidentally splash through a puddle. Now your shoes are covered with mud and soaking wet.

Wet shoes are no fun. Not only are they uncomfortable, but they can be slippery and dangerous in school hallways. Ask your teacher if you can set your wet shoes by an air vent or in a sunny part of the classroom until they dry. If you have an extra pair of shoes for gym class or a pair of boots, take off your wet pair and wear the dry pair.

At lunch, you find a spot next to your friend—and sit down on some jelly someone dripped on the bench. Now there's a strawberry jelly stain all over the seat of your pants, and kids are laughing and pointing.

It's OK to laugh, too—you love jelly, but not like this! Ask a teacher if you and a friend can go to the bathroom and wash up. Use water and a clean paper towel to get off as much of the sticky jelly as you can. If your shirt is long, untuck it and let it hang over the jelly stain. Or tie a sweatshirt or sweater around your waist.

Fashion Emergency Kit

These must-haves will come in handy when a button pops or your shirt gets stained. Store them in your locker or backpack:

- Disposable wipes—for accidental spills or stains
- Stain-remover stick—to treat stains and make it easier for parents to get them out later in the laundry
- Double-stick tape—to temporarily fix a hem or tame a collar
- Safety pins—to close a gap or broken zipper
- Adhesive bandages—in case of blisters

accessories

the extras

Accessories are the extras—the pretty earrings you wear with a sweater, the polka-dot bag you carry to the beach, and the sparkly belt you wear to the skating party.

Shoes, belts, bags, scarves, and jewelry—these are all accessories. They may be a small part of your entire outfit, but they can play a very big part in your overall look.

Accessories can help you make the same outfit look different every time. They can make something casual look dressy, or vice versa. They can give a new punch to something old.

Most important, accessories can help you add your own personal touch to every outfit. They're a great way to let your creativity and personality really shine through.

shoes & boots

Do you have a pair of shoes you LOVE? Maybe it's a lucky pair of high-tops, or a fancy pair of shiny shoes, or a bright pair of flip-flops that remind you of walking on the beach.

Shoes may be one of the last things you put on when you get dressed, but they can change the entire look of your outfit. How many of these styles have you tried on?

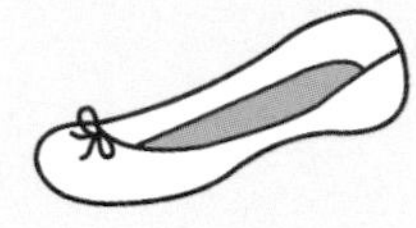

ballet flats

clogs

slides

Sneakers

high-tops

low-tops

slip-ons

lace-ups

casual

athletic

Sandals

flip-flops

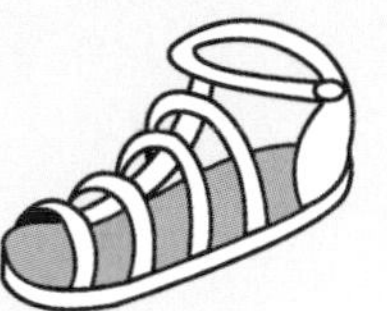
gladiator sandals

wedge sandals

espadrilles

Boots

ankle boots

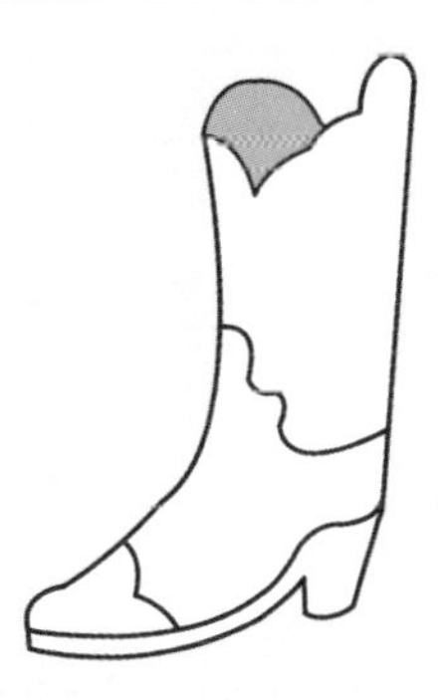
cowboy boots

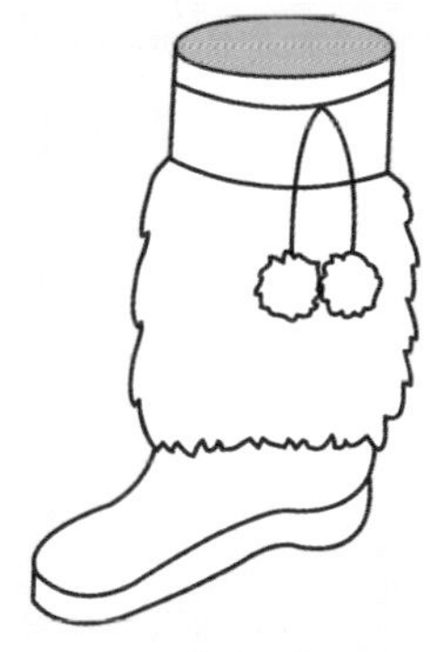
mukluks

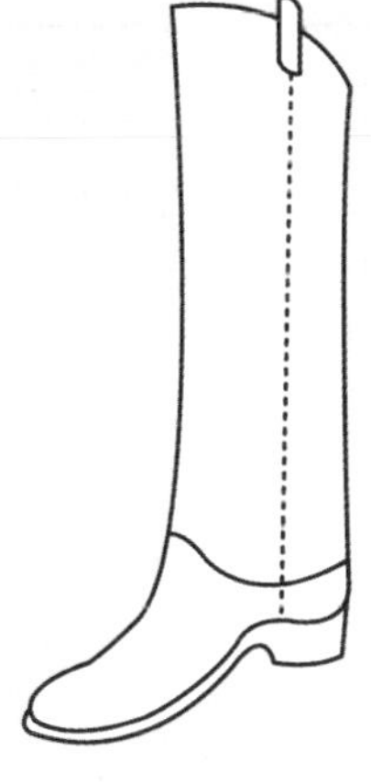
riding boots

Wellies

shearling boots

snow boots

purses & totes

Bags can be fun and functional. Which purse or tote should you carry? That depends on what you're wearing, where you're going, and whether you want to hang on to your bag or keep your hands free.

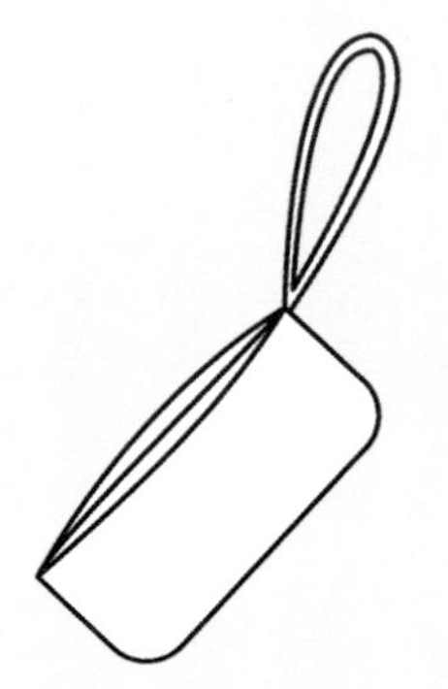

wristlet

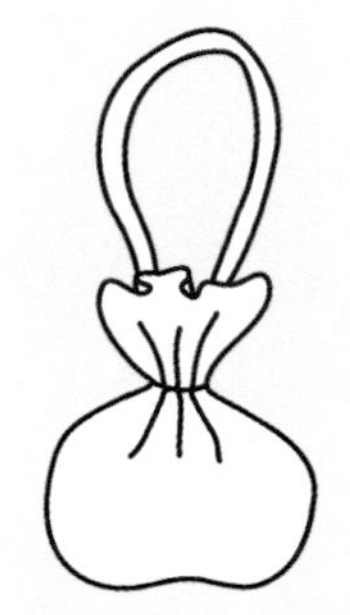

drawstring bag

clutch

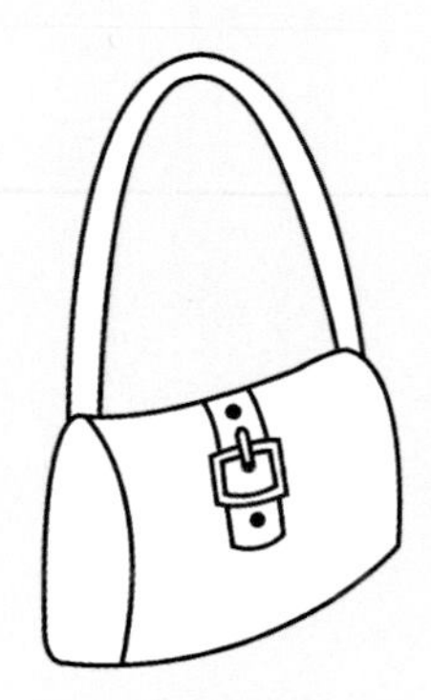

shoulder bag

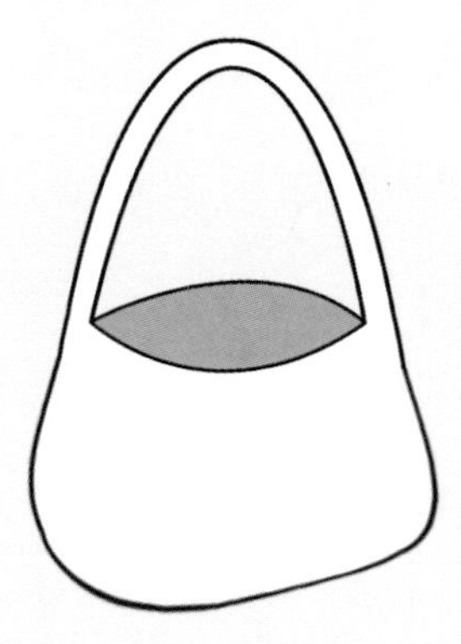

hobo bag

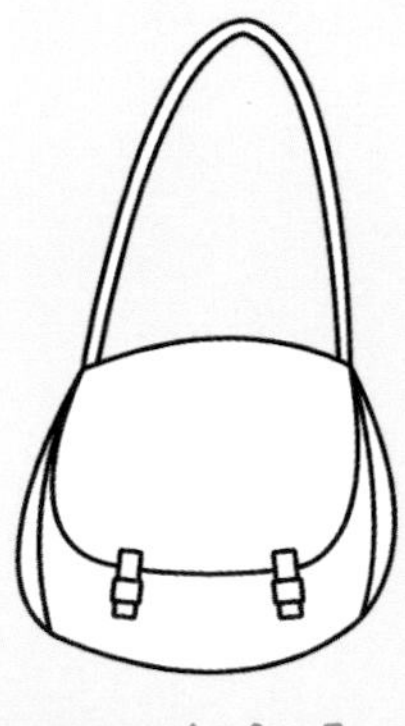

satchel

bucket

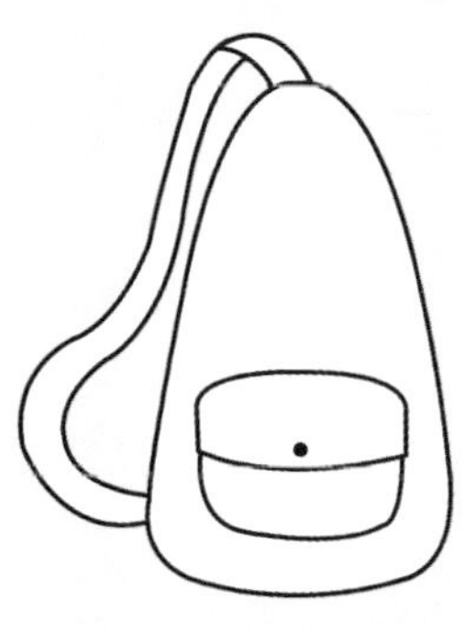

sling

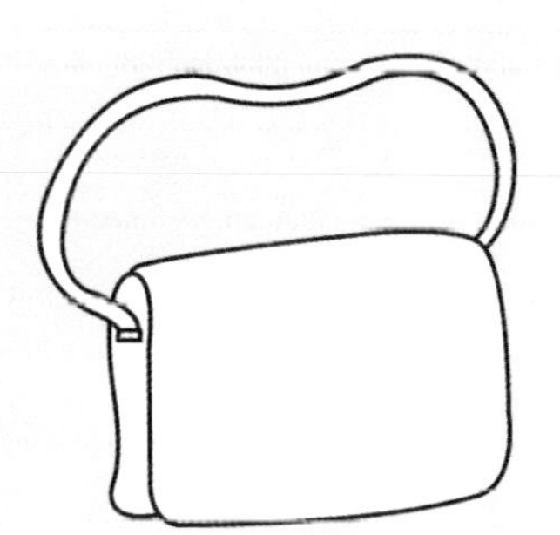

messenger bag

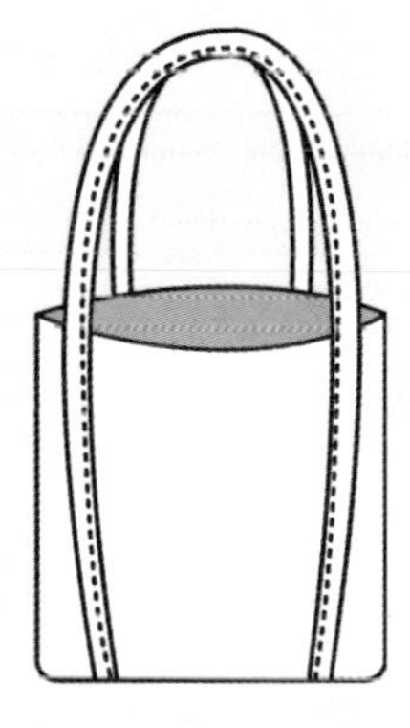

tote bag

duffel bag

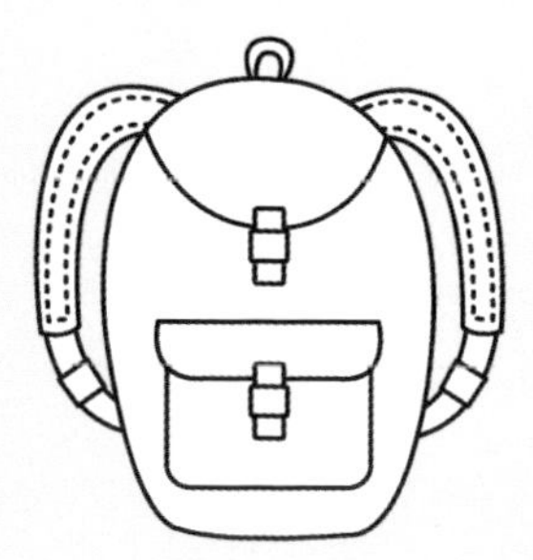

backpack

jewelry

Jewelry is like icing on a birthday cake—the sweet details that make a look extra special, complete, and personalized. Try some of these clever jewelry combinations.

String a ring. Put an oversized ring on a chain to create a new pendant.

Bracelet bonanza. Wear a collection of bracelets in different colors and styles on one arm.

Different dangles. Combine a necklace with another one—or even two or three.

Two for one. Wear a stretchy beaded necklace as a bracelet by doubling it up and slipping it onto your wrist.

Earrings are little things, but they can have a big effect on your look. Here's how to have fun with your smallest accessories.

Studs. Wear these small earrings on posts for any occasion. Choose fun shapes such as animals or fruit, or stick with stylish gold or silver studs.

Drops. These hang just below your earlobes. Choose a color that stands out against your hair color, or wear crystal or rhinestone drops.

Dangles. Complete a fancy outfit with dangly earrings, or wear them to dress up your casual clothes. If your hair is long, try wearing it up or pulled back. You'll show off your dangles and look extra elegant.

Chandeliers. These are the fanciest dangle earrings. They may be longer than your other dangles or have more beads or stones attached. Pair sparkly chandelier earrings with a rhinestone necklace for a dazzling dress-up combo.

Hoops. Small hoops are great to wear every day. Larger hoops will dress up your look. The bigger your earrings, the more they'll compete with other jewelry you're wearing. If you want to call attention to your hoops, skip the necklace.

Clip-ons. Even if you don't have pierced ears, you can still wear many of these styles. Ask a store clerk to show you some stick-on earrings, hinged hoops, or clip-on dangles.

hair accessories

Barrettes, clips, headbands, and hair ties—they're like jewelry for your hair. But hair accessories also serve practical purposes. They can keep hair out of your eyes while you play sports, and lift long hair off your neck on a hot summer day. They can be the key to a special hair design—that fancy bun you want to wear to your uncle's wedding. And they can be a lifesaver if you're growing out your hair or bangs. Try these stylish tips for holding hair in place:

Scarf. Wrap a pretty scarf around your hair like a headband, and tie it in a bow underneath. Or pull your hair into a ponytail, secure it with a hair elastic, and tie a scarf around the elastic.

Sparkly clips. Pull your hair to one side of your face, and hold it in place with a row of sparkly barrettes or clips.

Hair elastics. Pull your hair back into a ponytail, and secure it with several hair elastics spaced an inch or so apart. Use the same color bands, or alternate a couple of colors.

Bobby pins. Look for colored or decorated bobby pins. Use them to pull back your bangs or to add sparkle to even the shortest hairstyles.

Headbands. Wear two thin headbands at the same time. They'll make a bigger impact than one.

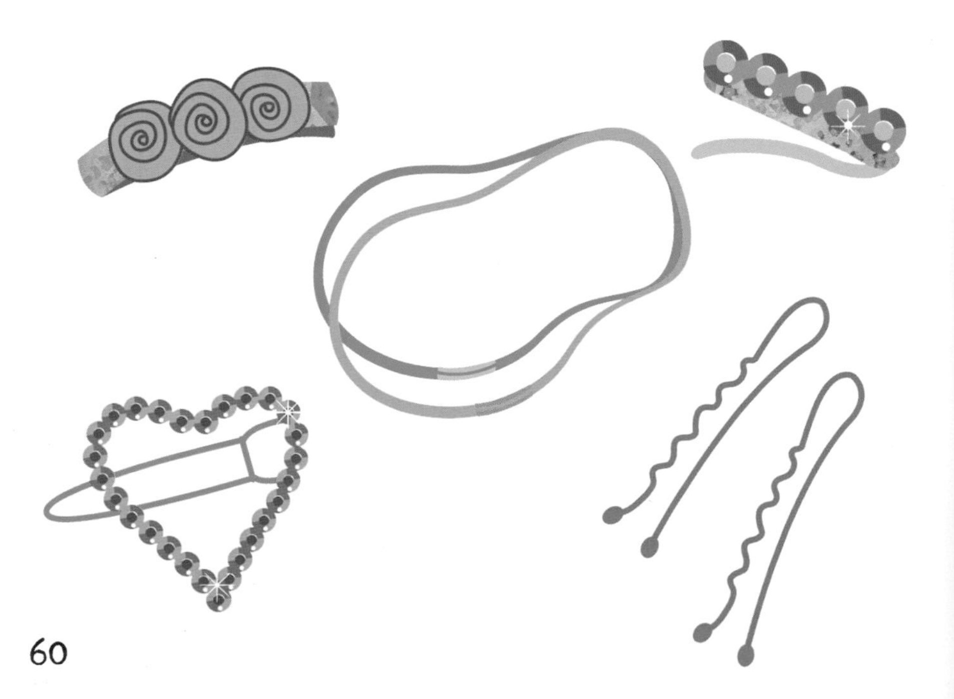

Trendy tip

If you're not sure how to wear hair accessories, ask an expert. A friend who performs in dance recitals may have a lot of experience with fancy hair accessories, or her mom might be able to suggest something that would work in your hair. Your hair stylist can suggest the best clips or headbands to use for your type of hair, and a salesperson at the mall might be able to show you how a certain accessory works before you buy it. There are lots of folks who can help you find ways to add flair to your hair. You just have to ask.

hats & belts

Hats can keep your head warm in winter or your eyes shaded in summer. When your hair is out of control, a hat can come to the rescue. And when your team needs your support, a hat can be the perfect way to show it. Whatever the reason or season, try one of these styles:

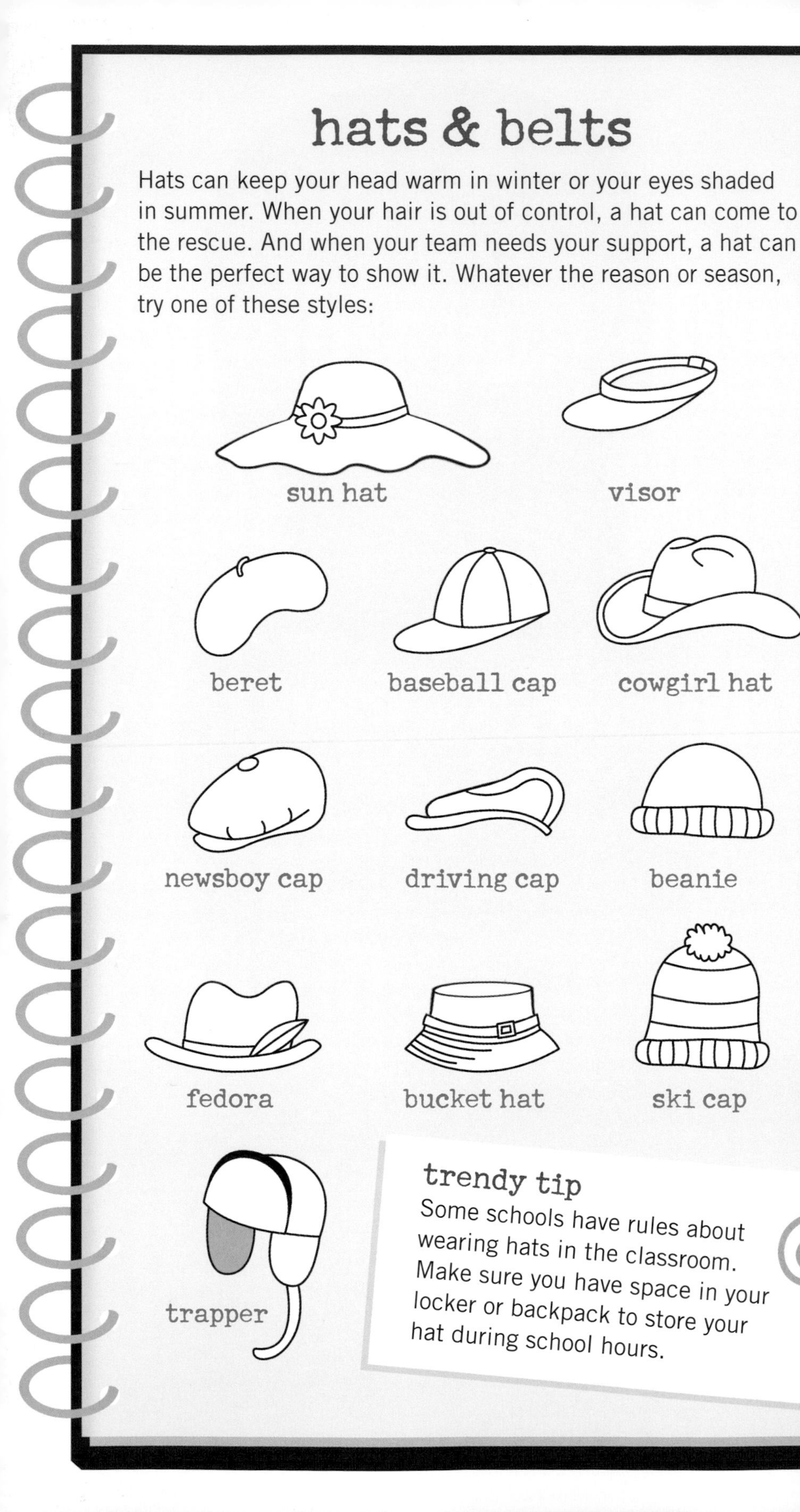

trendy tip

Some schools have rules about wearing hats in the classroom. Make sure you have space in your locker or backpack to store your hat during school hours.

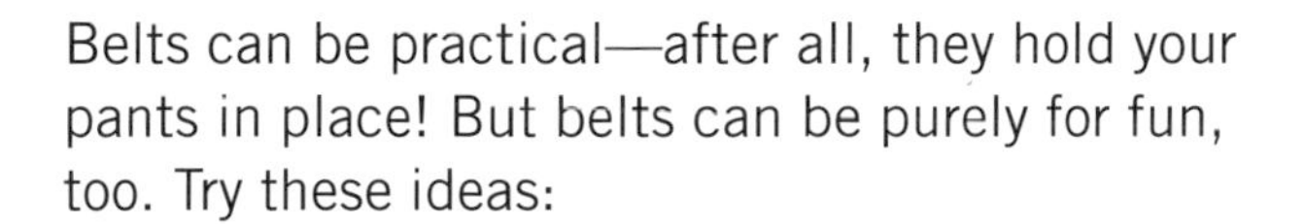

Belts can be practical—after all, they hold your pants in place! But belts can be purely for fun, too. Try these ideas:

Belt a dress. Add a belt to a tank dress or T-shirt dress.

Belt a sweater. Wrap a belt around a cardigan or an oversized sweater.

Belt a coat. Make your old coat look new again.

Belt a T-shirt. Cinch a belt around the waist of a long T-shirt.

Belt a belt. If you have two skinny belts, try wearing both.

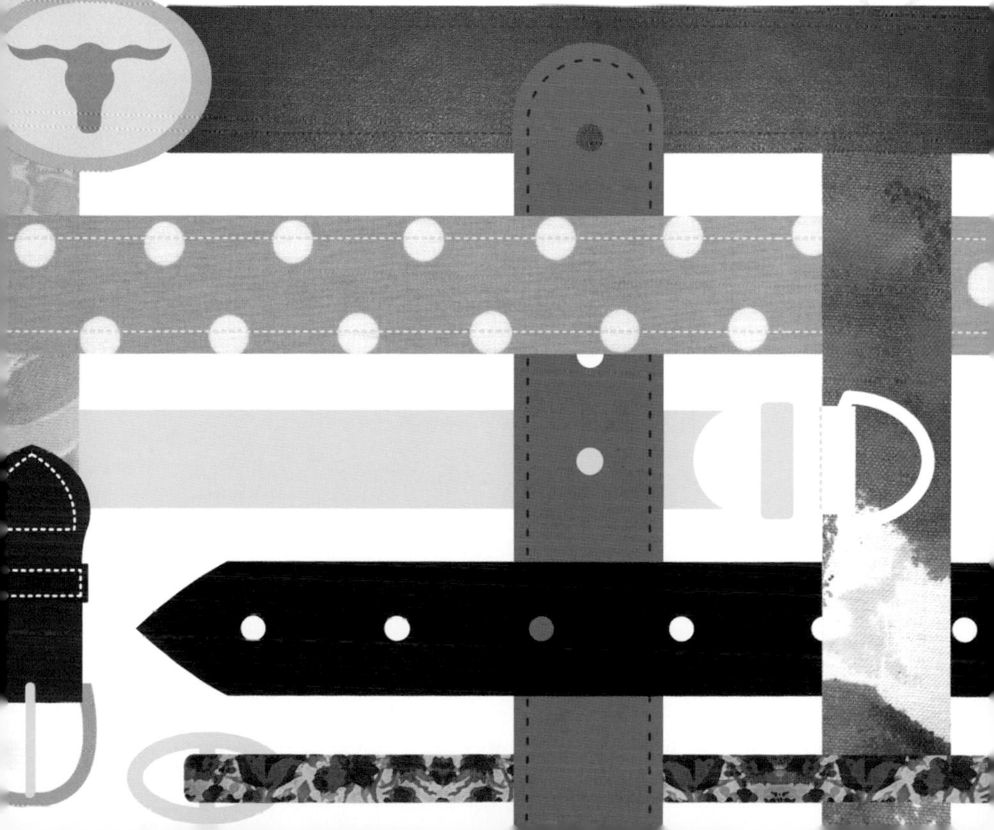

glasses & sunglasses

Glasses come in lots of frame shapes, materials, colors, and patterns.

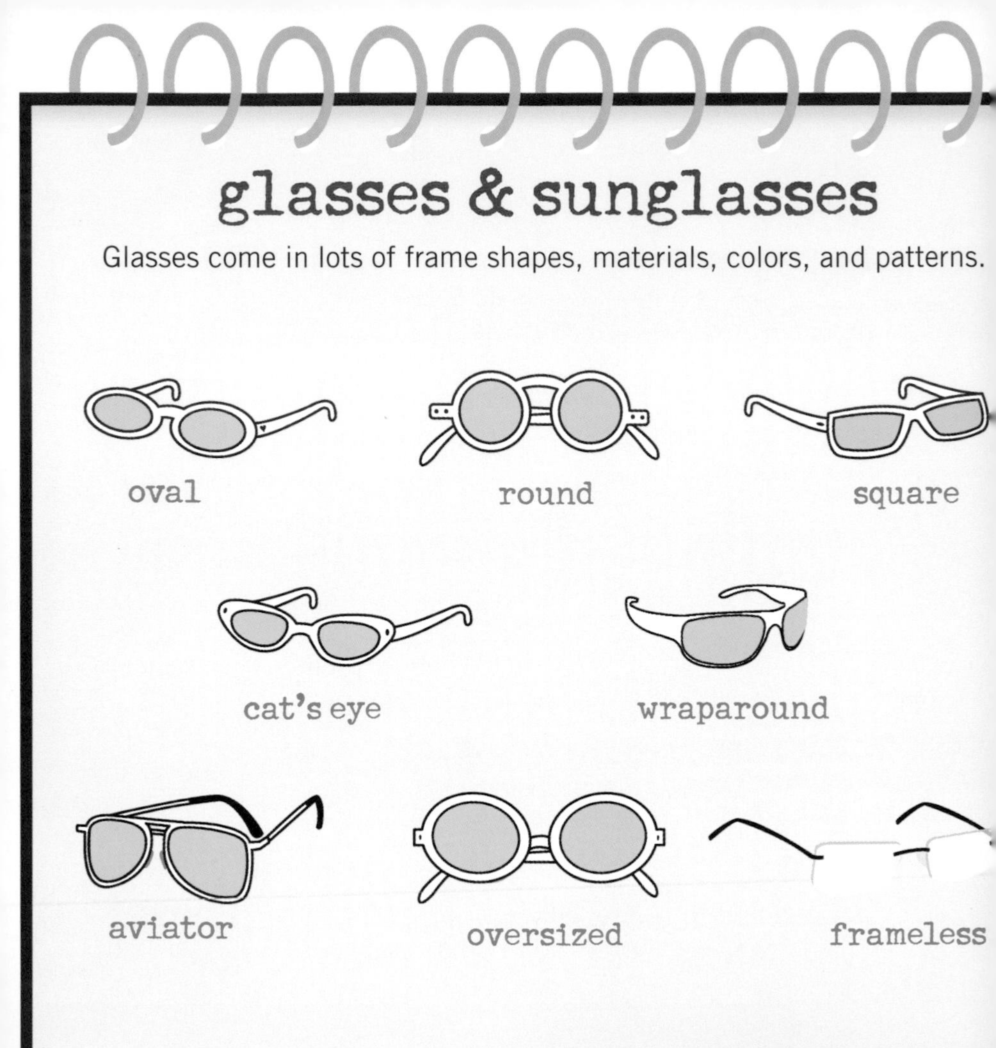

Choosing a pair of glasses or sunglasses can seem like a big decision, but it can also be a ton of fun. Follow these tips:

Find a girl who you think looks great in glasses.
Try to figure out what it is about her glasses that makes her shine. Is it the color? The shape of the frames? The way the glasses work with her haircut?

Invite a friend. When you're picking out glasses or sunglasses, bring along a friend whose opinion you trust. Have fun trying on all sorts of frames in different shapes and colors. Let your friend pick out styles for you, too. You'll be surprised at how great you look in designs you might have missed.

Protect your peepers. Kids' eyes are especially sensitive to the sun's ultraviolet (UV) rays. Before you turn 18, your eyes will absorb 80 percent of the UV rays that you'll get in your whole lifetime. When you're buying sunglasses, make sure to look for a pair that reduces glare and blocks 100% of UV rays, both A and B.

Stay focused. Being able to see well is the most important thing about finding the right pair of glasses—or sunglasses. You'll feel great when you discover how much better you can see the board in school or how much easier it is to view the world outside on a bright, sunny day. And when you're feeling great, you're going to look great in your new glasses, too.

Protect your purchase. Prescription glasses may come with a case to protect them, but most sunglasses don't. They can get scratched if they're bouncing around in your backpack or purse. Tuck them into one of these creative cases:

- a small cosmetics bag
- an old mitten
- a colorful sock

Trendy tip

If you wear prescription glasses and want sunglasses for outdoors, ask your eye doctor about prescription sunglasses or *transition lenses,* which darken into sunglass lenses outdoors. Or ask if there are clip-on sunglasses for your eyeglasses. Some attach magnetically. For a quick fix, throw a visor or cap on your head to shield your eyes from the sun.

six ways to wear a scarf

Think scarves are just for winter? Think again. Lightweight silk or cotton scarves can add color, texture, and style to your look all year round. And scarves can be worn in lots of different ways. Try a few of these:

1. **Belt it.** Pull the scarf through the belt loops of your jeans, and tie it to create a colorful belt.

2. **Cinch it.** Wrap a scarf around the waist of an oversized sweater or a dress. Tie a knot at the side of your waist instead of in the front.

3. **Tie it.** Drape a short scarf around your neck, and tie it loosely just below your chin.

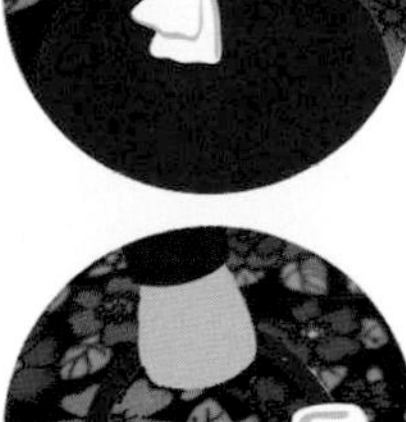

4. **Tote it.** Wrap a short scarf around the handles of a tote bag, and tie the ends in a knot.

5. **Band it.** Wear your scarf as a headband or ponytail wrap.

6. **Wrap it.** Wrap your scarf once around your neck, and let the ends flow freely on each side of your shirt or sweater.

Be scarf savvy

Scarves can be dangerous if they aren't worn carefully. Never wear a scarf that is long enough to dangle around your legs or feet, which might make you trip. Wrap your scarf loosely around your neck—never in a tight knot. And when you're on the playground, riding your bike, or skateboarding, a scarf can cause an accident, so wear a neck warmer or turtleneck instead.

putting it together

Bangles, belts, scarves, and sunglasses—accessorizing is so much fun, it's hard to know when to stop. If you worry you might be going overboard, follow these tips.

Keep it coordinated.
If you're wearing mostly silver bangles, choose a necklace with a silver chain, too. If your belt is brown, pair it with your brown sandals or tan canvas shoes. If you're wearing a pink hair clip, choose pink earrings. Don't have any? Try pearls or clear rhinestones—they match any color.

Think about size.
Are you wearing a **big,** fluffy scarf with a **super-wide** headband and an **oversized** tote bag on your shoulder? Too many large accessories might weigh you down and compete for attention. Strike a balance by focusing on one standout piece, such as your big, fluffy scarf, and complement it with a cute strapped purse and thin headband.

Check your clothes.
Accessories are meant to make your outfit more interesting. If what you're wearing is already loaded with personality—such as your animal print T-shirt or a dress with a big, bold pattern—you don't need to add much more. Save printed headbands and multicolored bracelets for the days when you're wearing solid-colored clothes.

Take one off.
For formal occasions, less can be more. When you're giving yourself a final check in the mirror, think about taking off one accessory. Chances are, you'll look more coordinated—and elegant—without it.

quick change

Want to dress up your casual clothes so that you can wear them to a party or a nice restaurant? Or do you want to dress down your fancier clothes so that you can wear them often—not just for special occasions? Here's how.

To go from dressy to casual, try . . .

- a **jean jacket** over a skirt or dress.
- **leggings** or jeans under your dress.
- a pair of **flats** or **flip-flops.**
- a plain **T-shirt** under your cardigan sweater.

To go from casual to dressy, try . . .

- **jewelry**—a dash of sparkle around your finger, wrist, or neck.
- a **fancy tank top** under a sweater or with your jeans.
- shoes with a higher **heel.** They give your whole outfit a boost.
- a pretty **hair ribbon** or sparkly **headband.**

Ask Mom first. There may be some items from your closet that are off-limits when it comes to everyday wear and tear. Ask a parent's permission before you wear one of your dressier pieces.

what do you do?

Need help with your hair? In a style slump? Accessories to the rescue!

Your parents are driving you to a birthday party in just a few minutes, but your hair suddenly has a mind of its own. It's going in all directions, and none of your usual clips or headbands seem to be helping.
Before you get too frustrated, look around and see if there's another option besides your usual hair accessories. Grab a cute beret or baseball cap to hide your untamed hair. Or tie a bright bandanna or scarf around your hair like a headband. Your friends' eyes will be drawn to the scarf, which means they won't be looking at your hair.

You don't mind wearing your school uniform, but sometimes you wish you could express your own style without breaking school rules.
Instead of concentrating on the parts of your outfit you can't change, focus on the ones you can—your accessories. Try a new hairstyle, and add fun hair clips or a bright headband. Slide a few bangles on your arm. Carry a colorful tote bag, purse, or lunchbox. Or find some pretty pins for your jacket or backpack. If you're not sure whether certain accessories are allowed at your school, just ask (before you wear them, not after!). And make the most of your non-school time by having fun with fashion on the weekends.

You were looking forward to the school dance, but your allergies are acting up. You don't really want to stuff the pockets of your jean skirt with tissues. Don't let a runny nose ruin your fun. Instead of using your pockets, find a great purse to carry everything you need. Look for a small bag with a strap that you can wear over your shoulder. It'll not only look cute with your outfit, but it will help you keep your tissues close at hand. Wearing your purse as part of your look also keeps you from losing it—and keeps your hands and arms free for dancing.

Your family is heading to the city for dinner and a holiday concert. You want to wear something nice, but your mom is picking you up right after school, so you won't have time to run home and change. Instead of bringing a full change of clothes, pack your duffel bag with a few accessories and one or two clothing items that will give your outfit a boost. Wear a nice sweater with jeans and flats to school, but after school, swap out your jeans for a skirt. Then add a few gem-covered hair clips and sparkly bangles. A pretty scarf can dress up your look—and keep you warm, too.

express yourself

what's your style today?

Just as fashion changes from season to season and year to year, a girl's style can change, too. In fact, your style can change from day to day. Answer these questions to see what kind of style appeals to you right now.

1. In your opinion, the perfect outfit . . .
   a. **is comfortable and easy to move in.**
   b. **shows off your creativity.**
   c. **features a little sparkle.**

2. If you were going to a friend's sleepover tonight, you'd pack . . .
   a. **sweatpants, a T-shirt, and your baseball cap.**
   b. **the tie-dyed pajamas you made last fall.**
   c. **pink fluffy slippers and a satin robe.**

3. When you get ready for a school dance, the most important part of your outfit is . . .
   a. **your canvas flats for dancing.**
   b. **your handmade dangly earrings.**
   c. **your gem-covered bag.**

4. To keep warm, you grab your . . .
   a. **comfy hoodie.**
   b. **funky poncho.**
   c. **cute sweater.**

5. You don't like to leave home without . . .
   a. **a hair elastic to keep your hair away from your face.**
   b. **a lucky bracelet you beaded yourself.**
   c. **a tube of sparkly lip gloss.**

Answers

If you answered mostly **a's,** you're feeling **sporty.** Being active, feeling comfortable, and hanging out with your friends on and off the field is important to you.

If you answered mostly **b's,** you have a strong **artsy** side. You love letting your creativity run free, experimenting with color and creating your own fashion accessories.

If you answered mostly **c's,** you enjoy going **glam** once in a while. You have fun dressing up and letting your sparkly side shine through.

Of course, these aren't the only fashion categories around. There are lots of other styles, such as beachy, Western, or outdoorsy. There are even combinations of styles. (A pink warm-up suit might be glam *and* sporty.) You might like all these styles or different parts of these styles depending on the day. And that's a good thing. Playing with style will help you express your many moods and interests.

looks to try

Explore a few other styles, just for fun. How do these suit you?

Free Spirit

Try loose-fitting, layered clothes in earthy colors. Add leather sandals and lots of dangly jewelry with natural stones and beads.

Island

Wear shorts or a skirt with a tropical print, add a shell necklace or ankle bracelet, and step into your flip-flops.

Picture this!
Before you step out of one style and into another, take a photo of yourself in a mirror (or better yet, ask a friend or family member to take it for you). The photos you take will help you remember looks that worked for you and how you combined pieces to get them.

Romantic
Try a flowing skirt in a soft color, ballet slippers, and ribbons in your hair. Add a pearl necklace or pink beads around your wrist.

Western
Put on cowboy boots with a pair of jeans or a suede skirt. Add some silver and turquoise jewelry.

fashion inspiration

Where do you get your style ideas? Is your inspiration coming from:

a person?

Maybe there's a movie star or musician who always wears a hat. Or a character from a book you're reading who always braids her hair. Or a girl at school who has a great jewelry collection.

a place?

If you live near the beach, flip-flops and Bermuda shorts might fill your closet. If you live in the mountains, flannel shirts, fleece jackets, and hiking boots might be more your style. If you dream of a trip to Africa, bright colors and beaded bracelets might appeal to you.

a passion?

The things you feel strongly about can impact your style. If you're an animal lover, your T-shirt collection might feature puppies or whales. If you believe in saving the environment, you might wear clothing made from natural fabrics.

a hobby?

Skateboarding, surfing, acting, dancing, and horse-back riding are all interests that might influence what you wear.

an experience?

A concert can inspire you to dress like a rocker one day, and a trip to visit your grandparents in New York can have you wearing a trench coat and big sunglasses another day. Your experiences influence the kind of styles you like.

It's easy to see why every girl's style is unique and can change so often. Since no other girl has exactly the same combination of passions, hobbies, and experiences as you do, your style will always be your own. As your experiences change, your style will, too.

An Inspiration Board

Gather together the many things that inspire you, and use them to create a collage on a bulletin board. These ideas will get you started:

- Pictures of styles clipped from magazines and catalogues
- Scraps of fabric or wrapping paper in pretty colors and patterns
- Photos of you in your favorite outfits
- Postcards of places you've been or would like to go
- Hairstyles you'd like to try
- Words and sayings that make you smile or feel strong
- Stickers, fortunes, and any other things that are just so *you*

fun with friends

Invite your friends over for some super-stylish (and silly) crafts and games.

Bowls of beads. Supply girls with beading or hemp cord and bowls of beads in different colors, shapes, and sizes. Let each girl string beads to create a one-of-a-kind bracelet.

Creative clips. Lay out plain hair clips, small rhinestones, and jewel glue. Invite girls to decorate their own cute clips. (Hair clips that don't bend will work best.)

Mix and match. Make four piles of accessories: jewelry, hats and headbands, scarves, and purses and totes. Each girl takes a turn picking one item from each pile until everyone has items from all four categories. Give girls five minutes to "accessorize," and then take turns showing off your creative combos.

Tissue paper trends. Choose one girl to be the "mannequin," and challenge the rest of the girls to create a new outfit for her out of tissue paper and tape. Can the tissue paper become a bright mini skirt or tank top? An oversized bracelet? A belt or headband? A funky purse? Have each girl design a different piece of clothing or accessory, and then put it all together!

Runway razzle-dazzle. Are you ready to model your creations? Imagine you and your friends are fashion designers about to reveal the latest looks. Come up with a name for your new look, and describe it to your friends as you model it for them. Or pair up and have a friend describe your outfit as you walk the runway.

quiz

fashion critics

When others chime in with an opinion on what you're wearing, how do you react? Take this quiz to find out.

1. When your brother sees you in the dress you're wearing to your piano recital, he bursts out laughing. You . . .

   a. run back to your room, slam your door, and cry.

   b. roll your eyes and go change into something else.

   c. ignore him. You know that any minute now, your mom is going to make him change into dressy clothes, too.

2. Your dad looks surprised when you come down for breakfast in a yellow sweater, plaid skirt, and orange boots. "Isn't that a bit bright?" he asks. You . . .

   a. swallow hard and mumble that he doesn't know a thing about fashion.

   b. tell him that bright is in, but after breakfast, you swap the orange boots for your brown pair.

   c. tell him he's lucky to have a daughter to keep him in the know about the latest trends.

3. Your friend asks you where you got your new coat, and you tell her it was a hand-me-down from your cousin. She laughs. You . . .

   a. blush with embarrassment. Can everyone tell the coat is used?

   b. change your story and tell others who ask that it was a "gift" from your cousin.

   c. smile and say, "I'm into recycling."

4. A group of girls at school call you a baby because you're wearing a T-shirt with a cartoon character on it. You . . .

a. put your sweater on to hide your shirt, which you'll never wear again.

b. avoid those girls for the rest of the day. You decide that from now on, you'll wear the shirt at home—where you can enjoy it.

c. hold your head high and let the nickname roll right off your back. You like your T-shirt. Who cares what anyone else thinks?

5. At a family reunion, your grandmother comments—in front of everyone—on how grown up you look in your new wedge sandals and sundress. You . . .

a. turn bright red and spend the rest of the day avoiding relatives.

b. smile politely but take off your shoes the first chance you get.

c. say "thank you" and take the comment for what it probably was—a compliment.

Answers

Hurt by what you hear

If you answered mostly **a's,** you depend on what other people say, even when they don't know a thing about your fashion interests. When someone comments on your style, think about their intention. Are they trying to help you, compliment you, or hurt you? Then decide whether or not to take their words to heart. Work up the courage to take style chances once in a while, and make sure your look pleases the person whose opinion counts the most—you!

Embarrassed by the buzz

If you answered mostly **b's,** other people's comments make you self-conscious. It's normal to feel embarrassed when someone shines a spotlight on you and your look. It's OK to listen to comments, too, but always consider the source—and your own sense of style. If you feel good about the look you've got, let the comments go. If you're still not sure whether you should change your outfit, ask someone you trust, such as a friend or your older sister.

Confident in the face of criticism

If you answered mostly **c's,** you meet the critics head-on. You have no trouble deciding whether their comments are meant to help you or hurt you. You're confident in your style, even when others draw attention to it. In fact, that confidence is a big part of your style and exactly what makes you shine.

advice from girls

When someone makes a comment about your clothes, how do you feel? What do you do? These girls weigh in.

"If someone criticizes what you're wearing, just say, 'Well, I guess we have different taste in clothes.' Then walk away."

"When someone criticizes my outfit, I ask myself, do I like this outfit? Because if you truly like what you're wearing, the criticism doesn't matter—you'll wear the clothes again anyway."

"My friend once told me that I looked weird because of the scarf I was wearing in my hair. I was sad for a second, but then I thought, why should I be sad? I like it!"

"When someone says something bad about my clothes, that's when I just have to take a deep breath. Later, I laugh about it. I know I got worked up for nothing, because I LOVE my style!"

more advice from girls

"When someone criticizes what I'm wearing,
I say, 'You don't have to like what
I'm wearing. You're not wearing it.
I'm wearing it, and I like it.' "

"When I moved to a new town, lots
of people criticized what I wore.
But then some girls admitted that
they actually liked my style. People
even started to come to me
for fashion advice!"

"I don't wear clothes
to please others.
I wear clothes
to please myself!"

"Sometimes criticism is OK. If a close friend is just trying to help and she says something like, 'I think those purple earrings would go better with your blue dress,' then you can take her advice, especially if she has great style herself."

"Everyone's style is different. Just because someone doesn't like my outfit doesn't mean it's bad—it just means that it's not her style."

"I respond to criticism by saying, 'Thank you!' People might look at me as if I'm crazy, but at least I let them know that they're not getting to me."

"When someone says something mean about my outfit, I say something like, 'Wow, I never knew you were a fashion critic!' It's a good way to stand up for yourself without being mean back."

"At school one day, two girls came up to me and rudely asked where I had bought my clothes. I pretended I didn't know that they were criticizing me. With a straight face, I said, 'In a store! Where did you get yours?' They haven't bothered me since."

when parents disagree

Parents care about the way you look for a lot of reasons. They want you to be comfortable, so they might ask you to wear a sweater or change from shorts to long pants. They want you to look your best, so they might want you to save your worn-out jeans for Saturdays. And they want you to dress appropriately, even when you think the shirt they're choosing makes you look too young or stuffy.

From time to time, every girl disagrees with her parents about what to wear. Follow these do's and don'ts to get through those style squabbles.

Don't wait until the last minute to show your parents an "iffy" outfit. Tensions will run high if you surprise them with an outfit they don't approve of—just as you're running for the bus. If you think your parents might have a problem with an outfit, show it to them the night before you plan to wear it. That way, if they don't approve, you'll have time to choose something else.

Compromise. Insisting on wearing something your parents don't approve of will only make them feel more strongly about their decision—and disappointed in your behavior. Instead, talk to your parents about why the outfit is so important to you, and listen when they tell you why they think it's inappropriate. If your parents disapprove of your crazy T-shirt and you hate their choice in sweaters, find something you both agree on, like a fun vest or fuzzy turtleneck.

Never buy something you know your parents won't like. It might be tempting to pick up a sassy skirt when you're shopping with your big sister or aunt, especially if she offers to buy it for you. But purchasing something you know your parents will find off-limits will break their trust in you and be a waste of money. If there is something you aren't sure your parents will approve of, set up a time to go back and look at it with them. That will better your chances of coming home with something you'll all feel good about.

Offer to save or chip in some of your own money. If you want a new piece of clothing that your parents aren't sure about, offer to save up your money and buy it yourself. If you show your parents that you're serious about wanting it and responsible enough to save for it, they may be more willing to let you have it.

help!

My mom always buys me clothes I don't like! I usually don't tell her I don't like them because I'm worried I'll hurt her feelings. Even if I tell her what I want to wear, she buys me what she wants me to wear.
Can't Choose Own Clothes

If your mom thinks the styles you like are too grown-up for you, you can't change her mind. But you should have a say in what you wear. Share your opinion when you go shopping. Try, "I like these jeans because they're comfortable," or, "I'm just not a frilly person." Focus on the clothes, not your mom's taste, and you'll be able to compromise without hurting her feelings.

I always get a big puffy winter jacket and big puffy gloves. I look like a snowman. I hate it, but my mom and dad say I'm warm and it doesn't matter what I look like.
All Puffed Up

Your parents are right—staying warm is more important than looking cool. Can you compromise and find a jacket you all like? If not, maybe you can also get a less bulky coat and gloves for days that aren't as chilly. If you offer to chip in some of your own money, your parents may let you get things you like better than your puffy stuff.

My mom bought me new tights with lots of colorful stripes. I'm afraid that everybody at school will think I'm a dork if I wear them. But I don't want to hurt my mom's feelings.

Afraid to Stick Out

Do you like the tights? If so, wear them and show your style. But if you're just going to shove them to the bottom of your drawer, talk to your mom. She doesn't want to waste money on clothes you won't wear. See if you can go shopping together to find clothes you both think are right for you.

My whole family thinks my favorite color is purple, but I like royal blue better. My mom always buys me purple clothes. Tell me how to break the news to my family!

Color Confused

Sometimes it's hard for people to realize that as girls grow up, their tastes change. If you used to like purple, your family just thinks that you still do. Telling them you don't doesn't have to be a big deal, but be kind—focus on how much you love blue now instead of on how much you hate purple.

big truth

Your parents understand how important style is to you. When they were your age, they tried different styles and looks, too. Maybe your mom shopped for a special graduation dress or saved her money for a jean jacket she just had to have. They might have disagreed with their own parents about what to wear. So they understand why expressing your style is so important to you, even if it doesn't always seem like they do.

shopping

what kind of shopper are you?

Do you get caught up in the buying or plan out your purchases? Take this quiz to find out.

1. All your friends have the same kind of bracelet, and they insist that you get one, too. You . . .

   a. **buy one the next time your parents take you to the mall. After all, the bracelet is only $3.**

   b. **wait. It would be fun to have a matching bracelet, but you're not sure you really need it.**

   c. **don't buy it. You already have plenty of other bracelets in your jewelry box.**

2. It's October, and you spot shorts at a cute boutique for only $5 a pair. You . . .
   a. **find your size and head for the checkout line. What a deal!**
   b. **wait until after you finish the rest of your shopping and see if you have money left over. They are a great price.**
   c. **decide to pass. You probably won't wear the shorts until next summer, and you don't know what size you'll need then.**

3. You're getting an award at the sports banquet and want a new dress to wear for the occasion. The one you love costs $45, but you have only $12 in your wallet. You . . .
   a. **look on every clearance rack until you find a dress that's only $10. You just have to have something new.**
   b. **decide to borrow a friend's dress and spend your $12 on a new necklace and bracelet set.**
   c. **find something in your closet that will work instead. You'd rather save your money for the dress you really want.**

4. You've got $20, and you want to buy something to wear on your beach vacation. You . . .

   a. **scour the store to see what screams "Surf's up!"**
   b. **choose new flip-flops because you grew out of your old ones. You splurge on a pair of sunglasses, too.**
   c. **buy a new tank top, which you really need, and then save the leftover money for your vacation.**

5. When you're shopping with your friend and her mother, they find a sweater that they think looks fantastic on you! You don't really need a new sweater. You . . .
   a. **buy it anyway. Your friend has a good eye for these things.**
   b. **agree with your friend, but decide to come back next week and see if the sweater is on sale.**
   c. **thank your friend but decide to pass on the sweater. You have one a lot like it at home.**

Answers

Sophie Spender

If you answered mostly **a's,** you love to shop and spot good bargains, but sometimes a good deal or the excitement of a new outfit takes over your own good sense. Don't give up on bargains, but try to think hard before you give up your cash. Make sure you spend your money only on the items you truly need or like.

Middle-of-the-Road Maddie

If you answered mostly **b's,** you like to shop, but you're pretty good at separating what you need from what you want. You try to find a balance between pouncing on a purchase and passing when something's not a perfect fit. You also know that it's OK to splurge sometimes on something you *really* like.

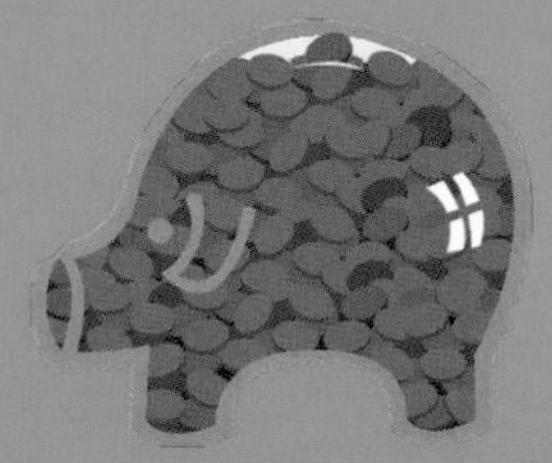

Sadie Save-a-Lot

If you answered mostly **c's,** you are careful about letting go of your money. You plan your purchases and hardly ever let anyone talk you into something that you aren't sure of. Spending cautiously is smart. Just remember that if you're smart with your money most of the time, it's OK to make a fun purchase once in a while, especially when you find just the right thing.

shopping buddies

Shopping is usually fun, but it can be twice as nice with a friend. Bringing along another girl who shares your interest in fashion and likes to try new styles can help you explore new styles, too. But a good shopping buddy is more than just a friend who likes fashion. She is:

honest. She never tells you something looks good on you if it doesn't. And you know she means it when she says you've found a perfect fit.

positive. She points out your best features and helps you find styles that complement them.

interested in your ideas. She respects your style, even if it's different from hers.

open to trying different things. She doesn't stick to just one style or fashion rule. She likes to mix things up.

budgeting

You want a new swimsuit for camp, new jeans for school, and cute new flats you saw at the store. Not sure you have enough cash? Talk to your parents about how much you have to spend. Then follow these tips to s-t-r-e-t-c-h those dollars and get more for your money.

Make a list of wants and needs. If you're wearing a hole in your jeans, you probably NEED a new pair. But you also WANT a new pair of earrings. Separating your list into what you want versus what you really need will help you balance your budget and your wardrobe.

Do some research. How much does a windbreaker cost? Look in sale flyers for prices, or have your mom help you search the Internet. Find out how much you need to save so that you're prepared.

Spend a little, save a little. When you get your allowance or money as a birthday gift, save half for your fashion purchases. Your savings will add up, and you'll find that meeting your goal isn't as hard as you thought.

Stick to it. It can be tempting to spend more cash than you planned once you're in the whirlwind of buying, but don't. If you've done your research, you know what you need (and what you don't), and you know what price is fair.

Plan around sales. Clothing is discounted soon after the season begins. Sweaters that appear in stores in early October will probably go on sale by the middle of the month, and prices may continue to drop until the season is over. Look for the sale racks at the back of the store. If you have your eye on something that's not on sale, ask the store clerk if she knows of any sales coming up. Also check your local newspaper for deals and coupons. If you've just missed a big sale, ask if there are any leftover sale items or online specials that you can check out with your parents.

Spend less on trends. It's OK to invest a little more money in a pair of gym shoes you'll wear each week or a purse you'll use almost every day. But spend less on trendy items that will go out of style quickly. Buy trendy clothes at discount stores, and choose smaller pieces, like jewelry and tights, to stretch your budget.

Think thrifty. Your money will go a lot further if you shop at resale stores. Secondhand stores are a great place to find basics, like T-shirts, as well as one-of-a-kind items. Wondering just how much you can save? Head to a secondhand store and put together an outfit. Check the price tags to see how much it would cost. Then do the same thing with a similar outfit at a department store. Do the math and subtract the cost of the first outfit from the second. Surprised?

Talk to your parents about your goals. Parents have a lot of experience with budgets. They'll be happy to help you stretch the value of your dollar. Plus, when they see you managing money responsibly, they'll be more likely to trust you to make your own buying decisions.

bargains

Sale! Reduced! Clearance! Bargain hunting can be a blast and a great way to stretch your fashion budget. But not all sales are what they seem to be. Remember, a really good deal means a fair price for quality clothing. Before you get wrapped up in the excitement of a bargain, do a little checking.

Check the original price. Some stores will put a high price tag on their merchandise just so that they can mark it down and make it look like a bargain. Was the original price fair to begin with? If it wasn't, then the discounted price might not be much of a deal.

Check the quality. A $5 T-shirt is a great deal if the shirt is high-quality, but if there are threads hanging off and uneven stitching—or if the shirt will fall apart after one wash—you'll be paying too much. Feel the fabric, look over the shirt for flaws or damage, and compare it to similar garments to decide if the quality is worth the price.

Check your list. You're shopping for sandals, but you find a great tank top for $2 instead. Often you run into bargains when you're really looking for something else. Pull out your list to remind yourself of the things you really need. If you don't need the sale items, you'll end up spending more money on clothes—not less.

Discount Downfalls

Big, bright, colorful signs catch your eye, but paying attention to the fine print is more important. Understand these common discounts before you flip over a deal.

Buy one, get one at a discount. This can be great if you actually need two or more of whatever is on sale. If you don't, buy only one—and save the rest of your money for something you do need.

20%–50% off original price. Sounds good, right? But is the price on the tag the original price, or is it already marked down to the sale price? If you don't know, ask.

Sale this shelf only. The sign may be big, but the collection of clearance items may be small. Figure out which racks, shelves, or bins are clearance areas before you get too excited. And look closely at the tags. Sometimes shoppers put sale items back on the wrong racks.

75% off select items. This sign might hang over a giant rack of clothing, but only some of the pieces on that rack are actually discounted. Is it the ones with a yellow dot or blue stripe on the price tag? Read the sign or ask a store clerk to find out.

Up to ½ off! This means that not all of the clothing is half off. Some pieces may be discounted only 10 or 15 percent, which isn't nearly as great as a 50 percent savings.

tricks for trying on

Make the most of your time in the dressing room by following these tips:

Wear a cami. Even if you're wearing a bra, put a white or cream-colored cami over it. That way you'll be more comfortable if you're trying on clothes that are sheer or if you're sharing a changing stall with a friend.

Wear clothes that are easy to take off. Avoid lots of buttons, snaps, zippers, and layers. Choose something that comes off easily, such as a T-shirt, leggings, or a skirt with an elastic waist. Wear slip-on shoes, too. They will save you time and energy as you get dressed and undressed over and over again.

Choose changing stalls next to each other. If you're trying on clothing with a friend, find a stall next to hers. That'll make it easier to communicate and to take a quick peek at each other's outfits as you try on different things.

Bring shoes for fancy dresses. If you're shopping for a special-occasion dress, make sure you have the shoes you'll be wearing for that occasion (or at least shoes with a similar-sized heel). Your shoes will affect the look and length of the dress.

Pull your hair back. Long hair can get tangled and full of static when you're throwing sweaters and shirts over the top of your head. Keep your hair in a ponytail so that you can concentrate on the clothes you might buy. If you really want to see how your outfit looks with your hair down, you can let it down when you're dressed in front of the mirror and pull it back again when you change.

Bring extra socks. When you're trying on shoes or boots, you might want to see how a pair fits with tights or thicker socks on. Carry an extra pair so that you can see how those shoes really fit.

Wear plain-colored underwear. Choose a skin-colored bra and underwear. Panties and bras with cute prints or patterns might show through the clothing you're trying on and distract you from seeing how the outfit really looks.

Leave panties on when trying on swimsuits. You'll still be able to get a good idea of how the suits fit.

Hang up your clothes. After you remove your clothes to try on something new, hang them up. This way, they won't get mixed up with the new items you're trying on. And they will be easy to grab and jump into if you need to run out for another size or color.

Depend on friends, not mirrors. The lighting and mirrors in dressing rooms are different in every store. If a piece of clothing feels good but you can't get a good look at it in the mirror, step out of the changing stall and ask a friend or your mom what she thinks.

Take only two or three things into the dressing room. Gathering up six or seven things to try on can be overwhelming. Take only a few items into the dressing room. Once you've tried them, return those that don't fit before taking more. Put them back on hangers, and hand them to the dressing-room clerk.

Ask for help. Store clerks will be happy to get you a new size or a different color. The clerks know just where those items are located, so they can save you time searching. And they can often suggest another style or color to suit you. Remember, though, that clerks want you to spend your money in their stores. So before you let a clerk talk you into a purchase, get advice from a parent or friend.

before you buy

You're in the dressing room wearing something you're pretty sure you're going to buy. Before you lay down your cash, ask yourself these questions:

Does the clothing really fit? Are you sure? Test pants by squatting or sitting down. Test shirts by raising your arms out in front of you or above your head. Watch for pinching or gapping—signs that a fit isn't quite right. Ask a salesperson if you're not sure.

Is it what you were looking for? If you walked in knowing you needed a pair of jeans but ended up trying on a great jacket instead, you might need to rethink your purchase. Make sure you get what you came for.

Is it in your budget? If the price is more than you planned to spend, consider whether you can wait for item to go on sale, or ask the salesperson if there is a coupon available online or in the newspaper that can help bring down the price. If not, check around for something similar that's within your budget.

Are you comfortable? It's easy to get excited about a great look and a great price, but in the end, comfort counts—a lot! Itchy sweaters, pinching shoes, and scratchy skirts will make you regret your purchase. Close your eyes and think about how the clothing feels.

Do you already have something like it? Then maybe you don't really need it. If you own a dozen cute T-shirts, think hard about how different this one is from the ones you already have. If it comes in a color you don't own, it might be a great addition to your collection. If not, save your money for something else.

Does it require special care? Look for the cleaning instructions on the tag inside the clothes. Talk to a parent before buying anything that requires dry cleaning or hand washing, as those cleaning methods may require extra time and money.

Do you have something to wear with it? If you bring home a new pair of plaid shorts but you don't have a shirt that matches them, your purchase will be disappointing. Think about what you have in your closet that will go with the new item. Make sure you can think of at least two matching pieces. If you can't, put down the item.

shopping for school clothes

Gearing up for the new school year? Before you go back-to-school shopping, figure out what you have and what you need.

Check your closet first. Go through your clothes and try on everything. Try on jackets and shoes, too. What still fits? What's too short, too snug, or too worn out?

Make a list. Shirts, pants, jackets, and shoes are often the most expensive back-to-school items, so if you need any of these, put them at the top of your list. Remember must-have items for sports, too. Then add underwear, such as bras, panties, socks, and camis. Put accessories like jewelry and headbands at the end of your list.

Check online. Before visiting a store, ask a parent if you can visit the store's Web site online. You might get an idea of styles you'll find when you go to the store.

Plan your trip early. Most school clothes come out in the middle of summer, even though school doesn't start until the end of August or beginning of September. Shop early for clothes and shoes that you really need, while stores still have a good selection of sizes.

Stick with a parent. Shopping with friends is fun, but if you have a lot of shopping to do, it's your parents who can help you make the best choices and stick to your list.

Make a few trips. Don't try to get everything all at once. That's exhausting—for you and for your parents. Instead, take one trip to find shoes and new jeans. Plan another trip to buy a new backpack or hair accessories.

Keep your receipts. Make sure you hang on to all your receipts in case you find that your clothing doesn't fit right or isn't appropriate for new school-year activities. When you get home, try on your new items again to make sure they fit. Don't remove tags until you finally wear your new clothes, and return anything you have second thoughts about.

what do you do?

Your body is changing so quickly that nothing seems to fit.

You've been to four different stores, and you still can't find a pair of pants that feels right on you! Take a deep breath. It's completely normal to have trouble finding a good fit when your body is growing and changing. Start by shopping in stores with clothing just for girls your age. You'll have a better chance of finding your size, and the store clerks will have a lot of experience helping girls like you. Ask a clerk to recommend a style of pants that might work for you. If the sizes in the store aren't right, she may be able to order the same styles in tall or petite lengths.

Your friends are all talking about an expensive new brand of boots, and most of them have a pair. You'd like a pair, too, but you can't afford them.

First, decide if the trendy boots are really your style. Do you want them because you love them? Or do you want them because your friends have them? If you decide the boots are truly you, ask your parents to help you come up with a plan to save your money. Watch for department store sales, or check out sale flyers from discount stores to see if they carry the brand you want. While you wait and save, keep checking in with yourself to see if you still want the boots. You might discover that you don't, which will free up your money for something else.

Everyone loves the new skirts that are in stores this season—except you.

Just because a certain look is in fashion doesn't mean it suits your style. Fashion trends come and go all the time, and another style will eventually take the place of this season's skirt. Respect your friends' tastes if they like the look, but don't try to force something that doesn't work for you. Stick to the outfits you like and feel good wearing. Staying true to your own style is the best way to stay *in* style.

Your mom wants to come shopping with you, but you want to go with your friends.

Your mom understands that you want to be with your friends, but safety is her biggest concern. Besides, in many malls, children aren't allowed to shop without a parent during certain times of the day. Talk to your mom and see if the two of you can come up with a plan. If you want to browse with friends alone, maybe your mom can take you all to the mall and shop in one department while you and your friends shop in another.

The jewelry store at the mall has tons of cute earrings, but your mom won't let you get your ears pierced yet.

Every family has different rules about pierced ears, but that doesn't mean you can't have fun with earrings. Look for stick-on, hinged, or clip-on earrings at the jewelry store. Ask your mom if you can wear them until the time comes for you to get your ears pierced. Practicing with these types of earrings will help you prepare for pierced ears and show your mom that you're serious and responsible enough to take that step.

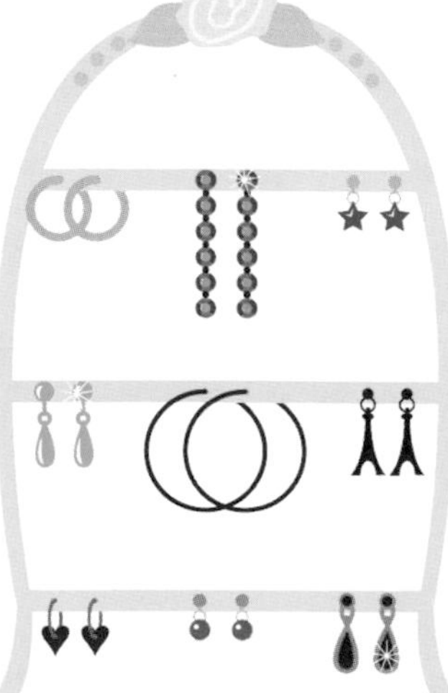

your
closet

closet boutique

There's a great place right in your neighborhood where you can find all sorts of wonderful outfits—at no extra cost! It's your own closet. Open it up, step back, and try these ideas for putting together some new outfits from your closet boutique.

Dig deep. Reach way back in there. Did you forget about that plaid dress hanging on the last hanger? Is there a pair of shoes stuffed in a storage tub or under a pile of magazines, just waiting to be rediscovered?

Get some help. Has a friend ever admired things in your closet that you overlook every day? Invite someone you trust to help you go through your clothes and pick out some different combinations. Sometimes a friend's fresh perspective can give *you* a new view of your collection, too.

Rearrange your clothes. Just taking things out and putting them back in a new arrangement can give you some great ideas. Try reorganizing your closet—maybe putting all the shirts on the left side instead of the right, or putting your shoes in a line along the bottom instead of stuffed in a basket.

Organize a swap. Did you find a few items you've outgrown or don't wear? Have a clothing swap with your friends. Gather together the clothing you no longer want, invite your friends to do the same, and then trade pieces. Make sure to ask a parent's permission first, and remind your friends to ask, too.

closet clean-out

Your closet is overflowing, and you can't find anything to wear. It's definitely time for a closet clean-out.

Pick a section. Instead of pulling everything out of your closet all at once, divide your closet into sections, and concentrate on one at a time. Choose the floor, your shoe bin, or your top shelf.

Pull things out. Once you've picked your section, pull everything out into an open space. Closets tend to be dark and cramped. Spreading out your things in a well-lit room will help you see what you have.

Sort your stuff. Try on each pair of shoes or piece of clothing. Does the item still fit? When was the last time you wore it? If you haven't worn something in six months, it's probably time to get rid of it. You've grown, the season has passed, and there's a good chance you aren't going to wear the clothing again.

Recycle it. Collect the clothing you've outgrown or never wear, and pass it along to a little sister or cousin. Or ask your parents to help you find a community organization that collects used clothing to help others. You may also be able to turn your hand-me-downs into dollars. Ask your parents if there's a resale shop in your area that buys gently worn clothing and resells it. Or set up a table at your neighborhood rummage sale.

Take your time. Reorganizing your closet takes a lot of patience and thought. Make sure you have time to tackle the job. Try breaking it up into several small tasks, and do one a day for a week until the job is done.

Trendy tip

Avoid hanging things in your closet that you think you'll wear "someday." This just adds more clutter to your closet and hides the pieces you like and want to wear often.

Once your closet is organized, keep it that way. Add:

- **labels.** Make signs out of heavy paper, and ask a parent to tape them to your shelves.
- **baskets.** Toss hair accessories, socks, and underwear into baskets of their own. Or roll up your T-shirts and stack them in a basket so that you can see all of them at once.
- **color.** Ask a parent to help you cover your shelves with colorful paper or fabric.
- **inspiration.** Find pictures of outfits you love in magazines and catalogues. Clip out the pictures, and use them to make a collage. Then hang the collage inside your closet, where you'll see it while you're picking out your clothes.

borrowing . . .

Your friend has the perfect skirt for you to wear to the school dance. Your mom has mittens and a scarf that would look great at the ice-skating rink. Borrowing clothing from friends and relatives can help you solve fashion emergencies and save a little money. But any time you borrow something, follow a few basic rules, so that friends and family are more likely to let you borrow clothing again the *next* time you ask.

Explain the details. If you're borrowing a sweater from a friend to wear to a party, make sure you don't end up wearing it when you go ice-skating, sledding, to the movies, and to church. If she had known you'd be wearing it to all those places, she might not have said yes.

Treat it like your own—or better. When you're borrowing something from someone else, make sure you are extra careful to keep it clean and safe, especially while you eat or play outdoors.

Ask about cleaning. Find out how your friend would like you to clean the item before you return it to her. Some fabrics need to be dry cleaned, which can be costly and might make you rethink your decision to borrow that garment. Other items might need to be hand washed. And if you're just going to borrow a cute shrug or skirt for a few hours, your friend may not want you to wash it at all.

Be prepared to replace it. Accidents happen. You might get a permanent stain on a dress. A shirt might get torn or a jacket might get stolen. If a borrowed piece is ruined or stolen while it's in your possession, be prepared to buy your friend or family member a new one.

Return it with a thank you. Tuck a thank-you note in the bag when you return the clothing, or add a small treat or gift to show your appreciation.

& lending

It's flattering when a friend wants to borrow something from your closet. That says she admires your style. But just as when you borrow clothes, you'll want to follow a few rules before lending.

Be sure. There may be some special things that you don't want to share. That's OK. Clothing that is fragile, easily damaged, or has sentimental value should stay in your own closet.

Ask your parents. Even if it's OK with you, your parents need to know that you're letting others wear your clothes. There may be some items that they won't allow you to lend because they don't want to risk the chance of the clothes getting dirty or lost. Respect your parents' instincts. They have lots of experience in the lending department.

Set some guidelines. Be clear about what you're allowing when you let your friends borrow your clothes. If you've agreed to let a friend borrow a sweater for the weekend, make sure to tell her when you'll need it back, whether you'd like it to be cleaned, and if it requires extra care. If you'd rather not lend out the item, that's OK, too. Be honest and polite by saying, "My parents don't allow me to lend out my clothing," or "Sorry, I may need this sweater this weekend."

Check it over. When you receive your clothing back, take a good look at it. The borrower may have accidentally snagged or ripped it without even knowing. Or you might find a stain, and your parents will need to know what caused the stain in order to treat it. If you notice dirt or damage, ask your friend about it right away. That's the best way to figure out what happened, take care of it, and avoid hard feelings between you and your friend.

pack it up!

When you take off on a vacation, make sure you pack what you need—and only what you need. Follow these tips to travel in style.

Roll 'em. Instead of folding your clothes, which can leave creases, roll up your sweaters, shirts, and pants before packing them.

Bundle outfits. Don't just pack lots of shirts and pants in the hopes that you'll be able to make outfits out of them later. Pair up pieces ahead of time and pack them together, like a shirt with a pair of shorts, or a sweater with a skirt.

Think about your plans. Consider what you'll be doing on vacation. A hike might require comfy shoes, pants, and a jacket. Dinner at a nice restaurant might mean a skirt and blouse. Remember the weather, too. The temperature in Montana is likely to be very different from that in Texas, even in the middle of summer.

Pack light—especially if you're flying. Many airlines charge a fee for every suitcase you bring, and some airlines charge extra for heavy suitcases. Even if they don't, you won't want to lug a heavy bag through the airport. Pack only what you think you'll need.

Be choosy about shoes. Bring no more than one or two pairs (depending on how long you'll be gone). Choose a comfortable pair for sightseeing and a dressier pair if you think you'll need them.

Wear bulky items. Wear your heaviest shoes, and pack the lighter ones. If you're bringing along a heavy coat or jacket, wear it while you travel. At least keep it out of your suitcase. That'll free up space for other things.

Use your shoes. If you're packing an extra pair of shoes in your suitcase, save space by tucking socks or underwear inside. Shoes are also great for storing breakable things, such as gifts or a camera, because they provide a little extra support and padding.

Keep important items handy. While you're on the road or in the air, you may need your glasses, toothbrush, MP3 player, and a good book. Don't pack them in your suitcase. Put these items in a tote bag or purse that you can carry along with you in the car or on a plane.

There's no doubt about it—you've got style! And by now, you realize that fashion, clothing, and the way you look on the outside are only part of how you express your style to the world. Your insides count, too. Your attitude—the way you feel about yourself, your friends, and your world—shows through.

This isn't the end of your style search—it's just the beginning. Your style will continue to change as you grow, so embrace what's unique about it, celebrate the tastes and interests you share with friends, and keep exploring new ways to express yourself and what you love.

Remember, no one else has exactly
the same style as you.
So let it shine!

Write to us! Tell us how you express your style. Send letters to:

***A Smart Girl's Guide to Style* Editor**
American Girl
8400 Fairway Place
Middleton, WI 53562

All comments and suggestions received by American Girl may be used without compensation or acknowledgment. Sorry—photos can't be returned.

Here are some other American Girl books you might like:

☐ I read it.

☐ I read it.

☐ I read it.

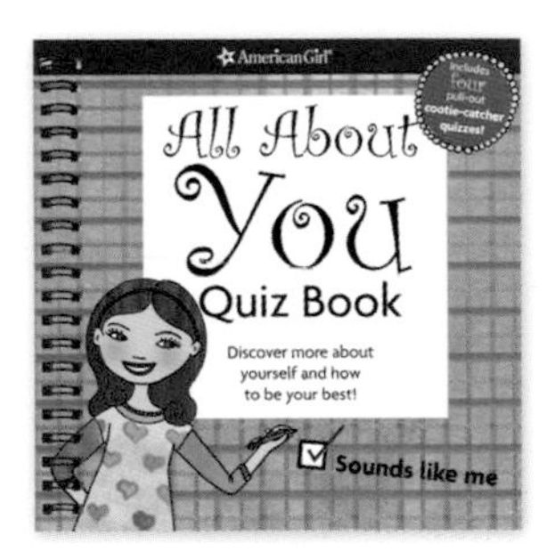

☐ I read it.

☐ I read it.

☐ I read it.